# YARN
# SUBSTITUTION
## MADE EASY

WITHDRAWN

P9-ELI-429

# YARN
# SUBSTITUTION
## MADE EASY

### Matching the Right Yarn to Any Knitting Pattern

CAROL J.
SULCOSKI

LARK
New York

**LARK**
New York

An Imprint of Sterling Publishing Co., Inc.
1166 Avenue of the Americas
New York, NY 10036

LARK CRAFTS and the distinctive Lark logo are registered trademarks
of Sterling Publishing Co., Inc.

Text © 2019 Carol J. Sulcoski
Cover and photography © 2019 Sterling Publishing Co., Inc.

All rights reserved. No part of this publication may be reproduced, stored in a retrieval system,
or transmitted in any form or by any means (including electronic, mechanical, photocopying,
recording, or otherwise) without prior written permission from the publisher.

ISBN 978-1-4547-1063-9

Distributed in Canada by Sterling Publishing Co., Inc.
c/o Canadian Manda Group, 664 Annette Street
Toronto, M6S 2C8 Ontario, Canada
Distributed in the United Kingdom by GMC Distribution Services
Castle Place, 166 High Street, Lewes, BN7 1XU East Sussex, England
Distributed in Australia by NewSouth Books
University of New South Wales, Sydney, NSW 2052, Australia

For information about custom editions, special sales, and premium and corporate purchases,
please contact Sterling Special Sales at 800-805-5489 or specialsales@sterlingpublishing.com.

2 4 6 8 10 9 7 5 3 1

Manufactured in China


larkcrafts.com
sterlingpublishing.com

Interior design by Nancy Singer

Cover design by Elizabeth Mihaltse Lindy

Image credits:  Photography copyright Sterling Publishing except as noted: Alamy: ©Grant
Heilman: 29 (Rambouillet); Christopher Bain: all yarns and swatches; Getty Images: ©Universal
Images Group Editorial: 29 (Cormo); Lynne Harty: all models; Shutterstock: ©Cole Eaton: 37
(bottom); ©Dr. Norbert Lange: 37 (top); ©Tony Mills: 29(Shetland); ©Nestor Noci: 21; ©D.
Pimborough: 29 (Bluefaced Leicester); ©Deborah Lee Rossiter: 42; ©Manfred Ruckszio: 39;
©Sponuka: 29 (Icelandic); ©Unknown Latitude Images: 29 (Corriedale)

For my aunt Jean,
with gratitude for her love and support,
and in memory of my aunts Carol
and Martha, who are deeply missed

# CONTENTS

# PREFACE

I wrote this book because when I was a newbie knitter, I didn't know how to pick out yarn. I would find a pattern to make and eagerly go yarn shopping, but once I got to the store, I had no idea where to start. After struggling, and asking for help, and making several projects that crashed and burned, I decided to learn about yarn substitution. It took me a while to figure out what I needed to know to substitute yarns successfully, but the knowledge that I gained has helped me ever since.

When I was asked to teach knitting classes many years ago, yarn substitution was the first topic that came to mind. It's a subject that knitters must understand to create projects they love. It's also a subject that isn't necessarily intuitive, especially for those of us who learned to knit informally. When I get to a certain point in class, I can see the light-bulb moment when my students realize how easy it is to substitute yarns once they have the necessary background—the technical information that follows in this book. Read, pick out a few patterns you've always wanted to make, then go forth and substitute!

# INTRODUCTION

The topic of yarn substitution is a big one, touching on many other subjects in the fiber world. After teaching about yarn substitution countless times, I've developed my own approach to what can seem like a bewildering subject. We'll begin by learning some essentials about yarn. Part I focuses on specific characteristics of yarn that will dramatically affect the substitution process: what yarns are made of (fiber content), how yarns are made (yarn construction), and what yarns look like (dyeing and other visual effects). You'll need a basic understanding of these subjects to differentiate among the many yarns available online and in your local yarn shop. The final chapter in the first section of the book is devoted to yarn classification, walking you through the yarn industry's system for organizing yarns into categories. At the end of this section, you'll understand *how* and, more importantly, *why* yarns are sorted into these categories, and you'll know how to select the yarn category that will work for the pattern you want to make.

Part II covers the actual process of yarn substitution, breaking it down into manageable steps. I've also created a worksheet to help you stay organized while you collect all the information you'll need to substitute successfully. You can copy the worksheet, then fill it out and take it with you when yarn shopping to ensure that you get exactly what you need—without blowing your yarn budget on skeins that won't work for your project.

Part III contains a selection of basic garment designs. Each is a versatile, classic pattern that you'll turn to time and time again—the perfect canvas on which to experiment with your own yarn substitutions. I've included swatches and suggestions to help guide you when picking your own yarns or, perhaps, to open your eyes up to new possibilities.

We've got a lot of important information to cover, so let's jump right in. The first step in successful yarn substitution awaits: learning about your yarn.

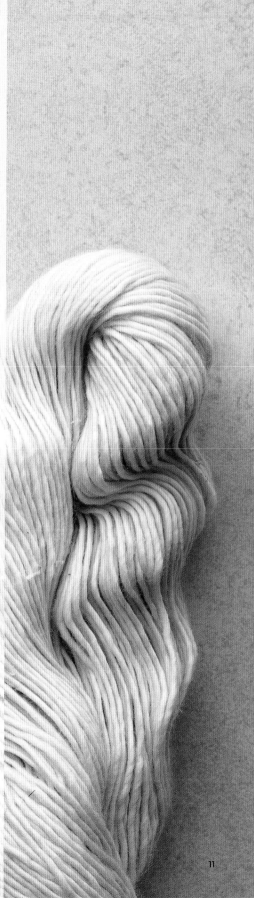

# YARN
# FUNDAMENTALS

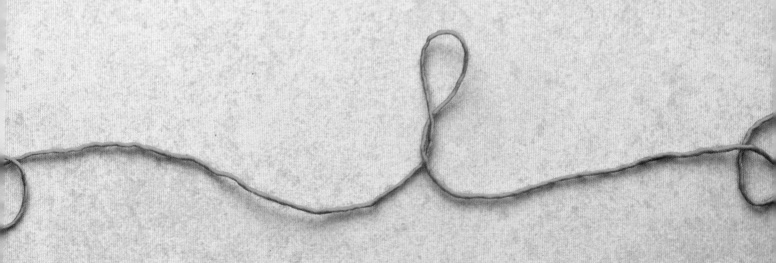

# 1

# THE BIG THREE: STITCH DEFINITION, ELASTICITY, AND DRAPE

et's start our look at yarn and fiber by considering three very important concepts that are commonly used to describe knitted fabric: *stitch definition*, *elasticity*, and *drape*. I refer to these qualities as "the big three" because they have such a significant impact on the appearance and behavior of knitted fabric. We'll refer to the big three again and again in subsequent chapters as we examine fiber content, yarn construction, and other key topics.

## STITCH DEFINITION

Stitch definition describes how easy or difficult it is to see the individual stitches in a piece of knitted fabric. Consider the two swatches on the next page (a). The swatch on the left is knit in a yarn that has good stitch definition. You can see each individual stitch clearly, and you can see the details of the overall stitch pattern clearly, too.

The swatch on the right is knit in a yarn that does not have good stitch definition. Because the yarn is fuzzy, it's difficult to see the individual stitches; the loose fibers around the surface of the strand get in the way. Those loose strands also make the overall stitch pattern difficult to see.

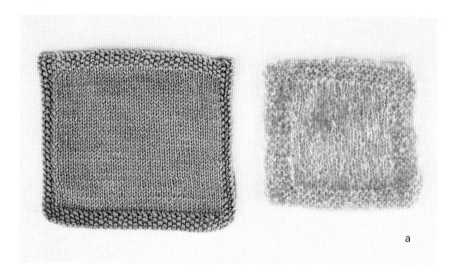

a

Whether a yarn has good or poor stitch definition is partly a function of how it's made and partly a function of what it's made from. Certain types of fiber, like mohair and angora, have an inherent tendency to look fuzzy, with fluffy loose fibers on the surface. (You'll often see these loose fibers called a *halo*; just as an angel is depicted with a ring of light around her head, so these yarns have a ring of hazy loose fibers around the yarn strand.) Other fibers have a smoother, sleeker surface, without short or loose fibers that obscure the stitches. When shopping for yarn, examine the individual strand to see how distinct its contours are: does it have a halo or a fluffy, fuzzy surface, or is the surface smooth and tidy?

How a yarn is constructed also affects stitch definition. Yarns that are tightly plied—made up of multiple strands twisted tightly around each other—usually have good stitch definition because the individual plies hold the yarn together, preventing loose fibers from escaping and forming a halo. On the other hand, yarns that are loosely plied, or that consist of a single strand of yarn gently twisted, are less likely to have distinct stitch definition. Because the individual fibers are near the surface, they are prone to fuzzing up from abrasion. Without a tight twist to hold the yarn together and tuck in the individual fibers, those fibers are more visible. This creates the fuzzy halo effect that results in poor stitch definition, especially with repeated wear. (b)

A trick of the light also contributes to the stitch definition that plied yarns tend to have. As we'll see a little later on (page 54), plied yarns have multiple strands of fiber twisted around each other. When the constituent plies are twisted in different directions and fit snugly around each other, they create a surface with many facets. These facets tend to reflect light and shadow, giving them a more three-dimensional look that enhances stitch definition. Yarns that are made of a single strand and yarns that are loosely twisted lack these facets, and this duller surface detracts from the yarn's stitch definition.

Sometimes yarn manufacturers deliberately create a halo when they are spinning a yarn. Many mohair yarns, for example, are spun in such a way that small loops are created along the main strand of yarn. The manufacturer then brushes out the loops, so that the loose fibers jut out, creating an intentionally fuzzy effect. Yarns processed this way are often described as "brushed," such as brushed mohair or brushed alpaca. Brushed yarns don't have good stitch definition because of their intentionally fluffy finish. (c)

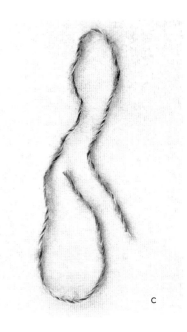

Why is stitch definition so important? Simply put, stitch definition allows your knitting to be seen and appreciated. If you knit a complex stitch pattern, whether lace or cables or twisted stitches, would you rather see the intricacies of the stitchwork or the yarn fuzz hiding your stitches? Stitch definition also contributes to a certain stylistic look—one that's clean, geometric, and precise. For less experienced knitters, good stitch definition makes it easier to read your finished stitches, so you can avoid mistakes (or catch them early enough to fix them easily).

That's not to say that less distinct yarns don't have their own unique style. Projects knit in yarns without clear stitch definition can have a cozy, fuzzy look or a filmy, romantic feel. Because these yarns don't show off complex stitchwork clearly, however, many knitters prefer to use simpler patterns and let the yarn's unique qualities be the star of the show. (Hence the old folk saying: "Either the yarn does the work, or the knitter does the work.") Of course, rules are made to be broken, and it's fun to explore the middle ground, experimenting by knitting more elaborate stitch patterns in less distinct yarns—you may be surprised and delighted by the result. (d)

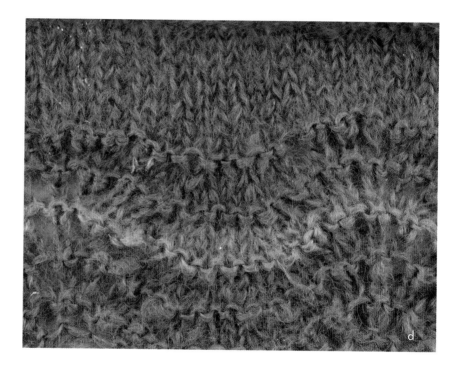

## ELASTICITY

Elasticity is the second of the big three and it's exactly what it sounds like: the yarn's ability to stretch and then return to its original shape afterward. Think of a rubber band versus a piece of sturdy twine. If you pull on the ends of the rubber band, it stretches out, and when you let it go, it springs back into place. If you do the same with the piece of twine, the twine won't stretch out or spring back. A yarn with good elasticity is like the rubber band, stretching out easily and then bouncing back.

> When we use the term elastic here, we're only referring to the inherent quality of a yarn to stretch and bounce back. We're not talking about yarn that contains elastic, a synthetic fiber woven with rubber that is added to waistbands to allow for a snug fit. (We'll talk about elastic in the fiber later; see page 20.)

Why does elasticity matter? Every time you work a stitch, you are slipping your needle into a loop of yarn and pulling the working strand of yarn through the loop. It's much easier to work stitches with a yarn that will stretch slightly as you insert the needle, then bounce back when you remove it. The more you need to manipulate stitches—whether you're stretching cable stitches across the front or back of the work, knitting decreases or increases over multiple stitches, or twisting stitches Bavarian-style—the better it is to use a yarn with good elasticity to make the stitch manipulation easier.

Apart from the fact that elasticity makes for a more enjoyable knitting experience, you'll find that the individual stitches in your finished product are more even and your gauge is more precise when your yarn is elastic. Compare the two swatches below (e).

e

Both swatches are knit in a ribbed pattern, but the swatch on the right is knit in an all-wool yarn, while the swatch on the left is knit in an all-cotton yarn. Because of the inherent elasticity in the wool fiber, the ribbing on the left looks crisper and neater than the one on the right. When the stitches are knit out of order to create the cables, the wool yarn springs back, but the cotton yarn tends to droop instead of snapping back into place. Over time, as gravity takes its toll, the nonelastic cotton will tend sag more and more.

Apart from the more pleasing visual effect, elasticity is important when you're knitting items, like socks or hat brims, that need to cling to the wearer. Elasticity means you can knit sock ribbing that pulls together very snugly; it also means that the fabric will spread out as you put the sock on and pull it over the widest part of your ankle, then spring back to its original shape and stay there, instead of remaining stretched out and saggy.

Finally, if you have any physical issues like arthritis or carpal tunnel syndrome, you'll probably find that elastic yarns are more enjoyable for you to knit with. Even knitters who don't have physical issues may find that their hands ache after working with very inelastic fibers, like cotton or linen, which require more strength to manipulate and don't have extra give.

If you'd like to use a yarn with plenty of elasticity, sheep's wool is hands down your best choice. Wool's structure (discussed on page 26) gives it built-in stretch. Most other animal fibers have less elasticity, often substantially less, than sheep's wool (although generally animal fibers have more stretch than plant fibers). Yarns created from plant fiber, like cotton and linen, are very inelastic, as is silk. You can easily see this for yourself. Try the rubber band/twine experiment with a piece of wool yarn and a piece of pure cotton or linen yarn. The wool will have noticeable elasticity, while the cotton has little or no stretch. (That's why there are so few all-cotton sock yarns; cotton's inelasticity means that all-cotton socks tend to sag and droop as the stitches are stretched out of shape but don't bounce back.)

There are things manufacturers can do to build more elasticity into an inelastic fiber. For example, blending a more elastic fiber with a relatively inelastic fiber, such as adding sheep's wool to cotton, can help. Some manufacturers add synthetic fibers that have great stretch, like elastic, to inelastic fibers to create a yarn with bounce (Cascade Yarns® Fixation comes to mind). Another way to increase elasticity is to use a chainette construction, discussed in greater detail on page 59. It's also possible to use stitches other than stockinette, such as ribbing, to reduce drooping with inelastic yarns, although this may not be enough with particularly sturdy fibers like linen.

## DRAPE

Drape is a quality of knitted fabric that is easier to see than it is to define. Fabric with drape is supple and hangs freely because the individual stitches are not firmly anchored in place but rather can move and slide by each other. When I think of drape, I think of the robes of the Statue of Liberty: they flow and ripple and collect in soft loose folds—they drape softly around her and form lovely waves.

Drape is partially a function of the type of fiber used. Soft, slippery fibers, like silk and bamboo, tend to create knitted fabric that drapes because the fiber's natural softness allows loops of yarn to move and slide. Likewise, inelastic fibers also tend to drape well (the flip side of not holding their shape). If you're looking for inherent drape in your knitted fabric, then consider silk, cotton, bamboo, and other plant-based fibers, as well as alpaca, or blends with substantial portions of these fibers.

How a yarn is made also affects drape. Yarns constructed with a flat finish, like tapes and ribbons, tend to have a lot of drape because of the yarn's flat shape and angles. Instead of nestling snugly together as rounded strands do, flat yarns tend to knit up with extra space in and around the stitches, leaving room for movement and flow. Yarn made with a smooth finish—like many extruded yarns (see page 60)—will also have more drape because stitches can slide past each other, while yarns with a rougher finish—nubbled cottons and loopy bouclés—will drape less.

Drape is also affected by how tightly or loosely fabric is knitted—again, because this affects the extent to which individual stitches can move freely or are locked into place. Knit on smaller needles and you'll have smaller holes in the knitting and less space in between the stitches. You may also have a fabric so dense it can stand up by itself! Use large needles and you create larger stitches with more space between and inside them. Less firmly anchored, these stitches can move and therefore tend to drape more readily. Thus you may be able to improve the drape of a given yarn, at least somewhat, simply by increasing needle size and gauge.

Keep in mind that drape is not necessary or desirable in every project. If you're knitting socks, for example, you don't want drape, or your socks will slide down and puddle in your shoes. A winter beanie also doesn't need drape; you want it to cling to your head and keep you warm. On the other hand, loose-fitting garments like a flowing jacket or a lace shawl that hangs in beautiful folds must have sufficient drape to achieve their intended effect. When thinking about drape, make sure to consider how stiff or clingy you want the knitted fabric to be versus how loose, soft, and flowing you want it to be. Then choose your yarn and needle size accordingly.

Remember the big three as you work your way through this book. I'll refer to these three concepts frequently as we discuss fiber content and construction; later on, we'll talk about how important these three factors are when deciding on a yarn to substitute for a particular pattern.

## WHAT ARE YOUR FAVORITE YARNS?

Find a piece of paper and a pen and make a list of your all-time favorite yarns. Include your workhorse yarns, the ones you prefer to use for knitting gifts, and the splurges that had you purring as you knit and purled with them.

Now make another list of the yarns you *didn't* like using. Include yarns that looked enticing in the skein but were unattractive when knit up, yarns that didn't perform well in the final project, and yarns that were just no fun to work with.

Now think about each yarn in terms of our discussion above. Which of these yarns had great stitch definition? Which were bouncy and elastic? Which created a flowing fabric full of drape?

Do you notice any themes? I've come to realize that I love yarns that have lots of elasticity and bounce—springy wools like Koigu KPPPM, Quince & Co. Finch, and Valley Yarns® Valley Superwash DK. Maybe you'll discover that yarns with drape make your needles sing, or that since you love knitting cables, yarns with good stitch definition please you.

Don't forget to think about the yarns that you didn't like, keeping in mind the projects that you used them for. Maybe you didn't like knitting a cabled sweater in a mostly cotton yarn—and now you know that the reason that your hands ached was because cotton is an inelastic fiber, not necessarily because you hate cabling. Perhaps the shawl you labored over just didn't look the way you thought it would, and now you know it's because the yarn lacked drape. (Keep those lists! We'll be referring to them later in the book.)

# 2

# FIBER CONTENT: ANIMAL, VEGETABLE, OR MINERAL

When I picked up my first pair of needles as a child in the 1970s, the only yarn readily available to me was acrylic. If you lived near a real live yarn shop back then, you could find wools and cottons, and maybe some silks, but by today's standards, a knitter's choices were limited. Today, a few clicks of the mouse or a trip to your local yarn shop (LYS) is all it takes to find wool, silk, synthetic, and cotton yarns, as well as yarns made from more unusual fibers—yak, bison, possum, bamboo, hemp, or angora—along with newfangled fibers, such as those derived from soybeans, milk protein, corn, or seaweed.

While it's fun to explore the many new and exotic yarns available today, to get the best results with your projects you need to understand why different fibers behave differently on the needles and in the finished garment. In this section, we'll take a look at the different types of fiber used in today's yarns, focusing on characteristics that will affect your ability to use these yarns when making a substitution. Keep in mind that entire books have been written about different types of yarn and fiber, and due to space limitations, we are hitting only the highlights. I encourage you to read and learn more about fiber sources to enhance your ability to choose yarns (see page 165 for some of my favorite resources).

When I was a kid, we sometimes whiled away the time on long car trips by playing Twenty Questions. Maybe that's why, when I consider the universe of yarns available to today's knitter, I divide them into three categories: animal, vegetable, and mineral. Let's consider them one by one.

## ANIMAL FIBERS

Wool fibers have overlapping scales, unlike synthetic fibers, which are smooth.

For thousands of years, humans have used the fur, fleece, and hair of animals to clothe themselves. Apart from their ready availability, animal fibers have many other qualities that make them perfect for clothing: they dye easily and well, they are good insulators, they are resistant to fire, and they are good at absorbing moisture and holding warmth even when wet.

No matter what species they are derived from, animal fibers are made of protein, specifically a type of protein called keratin. If you looked under a microscope, you'd see that animal fibers are covered in tiny, overlapping scales made from keratin. These scales help give the fibers their structure. The scales are larger or smaller depending on the species, and they may take slightly different shapes depending on which animal or breed they belong to, but generally the larger the scales, the rougher the fiber will feel, and the smaller and finer the scales, the smoother and softer the fiber will feel. These scales are also what make animal fibers so warm: air gets trapped by the scales and serves as an insulator.

### WHAT'S "WOOL"?

While most contemporary knitters reserve the term *wool* for the fiber that comes from sheep, you may hear "wool" used more generally to refer to any kind of animal fiber, or even as a general synonym for yarn.

### WOOL

Beloved by knitters for centuries, wool is frequently described as the ideal fiber for knitters. Wool is, as nearly all knitters know, made from the fleece of sheep. Sheep's wool is popular among knitters for good reason: it is warm, it absorbs moisture and insulates even when wet, it takes dye beautifully, and it is durable. It's a natural fiber and therefore breathable, biodegradable, and sustainable. Wool is widely available and plays well with other fibers. It's also versatile and can be spun into many different kinds of yarn, from tightly spun sock yarn to fluffy chenille to sticky Shetland wool for mittens.

Important for our purposes, wool has natural elasticity. Wool fibers will bounce back to their original shape and can be bent or manipulated without breaking. This natural elasticity and strength make wool an excellent choice for items that must cling to the wearer, like socks or hats, and for stitch patterns that require a lot of manipulation of the yarn—think cables, ribbing or moss stitch, twisted stitches, or lots of increases and decreases.

Alas, nothing in this world is perfect, and even wool has a few problematic characteristics. Some poor souls are, sadly, allergic or have a sensitivity to wool (or at least certain types of wool) and simply cannot use it. Wool has the tendency to attract moths, who love to chew it to shreds. If not processed correctly, or if poor quality wool is used to make the yarn, it can feel scratchy and itchy. And wool requires care in washing or it will shrink and felt.

## Breeds of Sheep

While we often discuss wool as a single, uniform fiber, there are over a thousand distinct breeds of sheep, which vary greatly in their individual characteristics—including the qualities of their wool. Think about dogs: there are scores of dog breeds that differ in size and shape, from Chihuahuas to Great Danes to schnauzers. Consider how different the coat of each dog breed is. Golden retrievers have a glossy, silky coat with long hair; poodles have curlier, somewhat coarser hair; greyhounds have very short hair. It's the same when it comes to sheep breeds. There are breeds with long lustrous locks, shorter coarser fleece, or curly or crimped wool; wool that has shine and wool that is matte; wool that is smoother and wool that is stickier; wool in every shade from white to brown to gray to black—and spotted sheep, too.

If you look at the label on a skein of wool yarn, you'll often see the content described as "100% wool," without any reference to the breed. When mills purchase wool, they generally focus on qualities like its fineness and crimp more than the breed of sheep that produced it. By purchasing batches of wool based on the qualities of the fiber instead of the sheep breed, wool brokers end up with a "homogenized" mixture. The exact breeds used to create the pool will vary from year to year, and the proportions of each breed within the pool will vary, too. One year, a farm with Corriedale sheep will have a better yield and so more of its wool will go into the mix; another year, that producer may contribute a smaller proportion to the mix while a larger amount of Columbia goes in. Regardless of the exact mix, the yarn is labeled as all-wool. This variation in the sources of the wool may explain why the same brand and line of wool yarn may feel slightly different from year to year. (It's not your imagination!)

For many years, merino wool was one of the few breeds of wool commonly segregated for the hand-knitting market. Merino wool, developed in Spain centuries ago, is highly prized for its extremely soft hand, fine fibers, springiness, and receptivity to dye. In fact, the export of merino yarn was strictly controlled by Spain to maintain its monopoly on this favored fiber, with unauthorized export at one time punishable by death! Thankfully, merino yarn is widely available today, penalty-free. Yarn made from 100 percent merino fleece is more expensive, however, to reflect its higher quality and relative scarcity.

One exciting development in the knitting world in recent years has been the increasing availability of yarns that specify which breeds produced the wool. Perhaps an outgrowth of the general trend toward small makers and artisanal products, these yarns are not made from a generic wool mix but from wool of one or two specific breeds, allowing the unique characteristics of the breed(s) to shine. For example, the yarn *Flock*, made by the company A Verb for Keeping Warm, is spun from two specific sheep breeds, Rambouillet and Targhee, while larger companies offer selections like Lorna's Laces Masham or Debbie Bliss Blue Faced Leicester Aran. Some working farms sell yarn derived from their own animals and offer unique cross-breeds unavailable on a larger scale; the Long Island Yarn & Farm Company can even tell you the name of the sheep or alpaca the fiber came from!

While all wool has certain characteristics in common, you'll find that yarn made from different breeds of sheep can knit up very differently from one another. Here are a few of the breed-specific yarns you may encounter when yarn shopping and some of their characteristics. I've included several sources of information about specific breeds of sheeps in the bibliography (page 165), if you'd like to learn more.

| NAME OF BREED | CHARACTERISTICS | COMMONLY USED FOR |
|---|---|---|
| SHETLAND | Soft, fine, wavy; comes in many natural colors; crunchy hand | Very fine-gauge lace; stranded colorwork |
| CORRIEDALE | Nice crimp; bred by crossing merino with other breeds; longer fiber than merino; soft | Sweaters; good all-around wool; felting |
| ICELANDIC | Longer fibers; very warm; often loosely spun | Yoke sweaters (lopapeysas); outdoor layers |
| BLUEFACED LEICESTER | Luster; takes dye well; similar in hand to merino | Socks; shawls; anything you would knit in merino |
| RAMBOUILLET | Similar to merino; very bouncy; crimp, slightly matte surface | Good all-purpose wool; works well when blended with other fibers |
| CORMO | Bred from Corriedale and merino; fine wool; lustrous; crimp; felts easily | Soft enough for next-to-skin wear but sturdy enough for other garments |

# WOOL-OLOGY

You may have seen some of these terms on yarn labels and wondered what they mean. Here's a glossary:

**Extra fine**, superfine, and ultrafine are terms used to categorize wool based on its micron count. The micron is a unit of measurement used to describe the size of the individual fibers in a yarn. The smaller the micron, the finer and softer the resulting yarn is. Extra fine describes fibers 18.6 to 19.5 microns in diameter; superfine is the next category, with wools from 17.6 to 18.5 microns in diameter; and ultrafine is the category assigned to the finest of wools (for the technically minded, less than 17.5 microns in diameter).

**Lambswool** is wool that has been sheared from a lamb as opposed to an adult sheep. Just as a baby human's hair is downy and softer than an adult's, a baby sheep's fleece is finer and softer than an adult sheep's.

**Superwash wool** has been chemically treated to prevent it from felting. Remember those microscopic scales made of keratin (page 26)? When subjected to water, heat, agitation, and soap, those scales undergo a process in which they meld together. The fusing of scales into each other is what we call felting. Once wool has felted, however, you can't un-felt it—hence wool's reputation for being tricky to wash. All superwash processes involve treating the scales on the yarn (removing the scales or covering them with resin are two common methods) so that they will not mesh together during the washing process. Superwash yarns tend to have a softer, less crisp hand than non-superwash wools; critics say that superwash yarn can be limp and lack some of the inherent elasticity that untreated wool has. On the other hand, superwash wools do allow wool garments to be washed with less possibility of felting or shrinking, which can be a very good thing.

**Virgin wool** usually refers to wool that has never been used before, as opposed to wool that has been recycled. It may also refer to wool that has been taken from a lamb's very first shearing.

## ALPACA

The majestic alpaca has been bred for its fiber in South America for thousands of years. It's small wonder, because alpaca fiber is incredibly soft, beautiful, and warm. Alpaca is a hollow fiber, which means it is a terrific insulator and even warmer than sheep's wool. Alpaca has long fibers with little memory; an alpaca garment will drape beautifully, but won't return to its shape if stretched out. The keratin scales on alpaca fiber are larger than those on wool, which gives it luster as the scales reflect light; the larger scales also make the fiber a bit more resistant to felting than wool.

Alpaca come in two breeds: the Suri and the Huacaya. The Suri breed is rarer and produces the finest, softest fiber, suitable for next-to-the-skin wear. Huacaya alpacas are far more common, but their fiber is a bit coarser and denser, with some crimp. Suri alpaca will be labeled as such, and you'll pay a premium since the fiber is softer and finer.

Like wool, alpaca fiber comes in different ranges of softness. Baby alpaca, taken from the first shearing of a young animal, is on a par with cashmere in terms of softness. Superfine alpaca is not necessarily from baby alpaca but is especially fine, and the grade "royal" is the finest of all (in the past, it was reserved for Andean royalty, but today it is mainly sold to the fashion industry). Because it has relatively long fibers, some alpaca yarns tend to shed.

Alpaca yarn and its cousins (see page 32) are great for garments where warmth and drape are desirable. Because of alpaca's inherent inelasticity, it's less successful when used in close-fitting garments and those that require lots of structure, but looks fabulous when used for flowing designs that take advantage of its natural drape. Alpaca is both warm and lightweight, so take that into account when deciding on how thick or thin a yarn you'll use. You may find, for example, that DK-weight alpaca keeps you as warm as, say, worsted-weight wool; if so, you'll need to adjust your project accordingly.

## ALPACA KIN

Like its cousin, the alpaca, the llama also comes from South America, although llamas were used predominantly as pack animals rather than for their fiber. Nevertheless, llama fiber has many similarities to alpaca, such as lightweight warmth, relative inelasticity, and softness. Like all large fiber animals, llamas have sharp guard hairs that can make poorly chosen fiber or inexpertly processed yarn feel scratchy. And as with most fiber animals, fiber from the baby llama is softer, more desirable, and more expensive than fiber from adults.

The vicuña is a close relative of the alpaca and produces even finer and softer fiber—at a premium price. Because the current population of vicuñas is so small, the fiber is scarce and therefore very expensive; it is one of the most expensive fibers in the world and a true luxury item. When they say that vicuña fiber is soft, they do mean soft: its micron count ranges around 8 to 10 microns (compare that to cashmere, which averages around 14 microns in diameter). Occasionally you may hear of the guanaco, a close relative of the vicuña. Guanacos are somewhat bigger than vicuñas, with fiber that is not as fine as the vicuña but finer than most alpaca. Guanaco yarn is a bit harder to find than alpaca but more affordable than vicuña.

## CASHMERE

One of two very different fibers that come from goats, cashmere is renowned for its fine hand, warmth, and softness—even George Costanza wasn't immune to its allure. Cashmere is a luxury fiber, gathered only once a year by combing the underbelly of a specific breed of goat, the Kashmir. Since these goats inhabit remote regions in Tibet and China, cashmere is expensive.

Cashmere fiber is fairly short and more delicate than wool, so it's often blended with other fibers (wool and nylon, in particular) to add strength and durability to the finished yarn. Because pure cashmere is both delicate and expensive, its best use is for items that get less wear and are worn close to the skin, like cowls, scarves, and shawls.

## MOHAIR

Mohair is also produced by goats, but by an entirely different breed: the Angora goat. (Just to make things confusing, mohair comes from the Angora breed of goat, while angora comes from the Angora breed of rabbit.) Mohair has a distinct sheen and reflects light beautifully due to its larger scales. It also takes dye very well. It is warm, lightweight, and strong and often has a distinct halo. Although not very elastic, it does have drape when not in a brushed form. Opinions differ about the softness of mohair, but apart from individual sensitivity to the breed, whether you find mohair silky and soft or scratchy and rough depends greatly on the grade of the fiber and how it is processed. The softest grade of mohair is superfine kid mohair, which comes from the first shearing of the youngest animals; kid mohair is next softest; and so on, with adult mohair being the least fine grade and therefore the least soft. Because you'll pay a premium for the finer grades, descriptors like "baby" or "kid" are generally listed right on the label.

Lately more companies have been experimenting with yarns that contain a good percentage of mohair but are not brushed or put into bouclé form. Quince & Co., for example, has introduced a yarn called Piper, which consists of 50 percent superfine kid mohair and 50 percent superfine merino, and the resulting yarn is lovely. Personally, I prefer mohair as part of a blend of yarns. The mohair content gives the yarn sheen, while the dye adheres to the different constituent fibers in slightly different ways, giving even a solid color extra complexity. Brushed mohair is often mixed with silk, as in Rowan's perennial favorite, Kidsilk Haze; often nylon is added to the mix to hold it all together. Mohair/silk blends are often used as carry-along yarns to add haze and shine to other yarns.

Because of its drape, mohair is excellent for cowls, scarves, and shawls, as well as flowing jackets and wraps. You'll want to consider the yarn's halo, especially if you're using a brushed mohair, when deciding on a stitch pattern, so that you balance the yarn's haziness with the complexity of your stitchwork.

## YAK, BISON, AND OTHER LARGE BEASTS

As ranchers turn to animals that are not in most renditions of "Old Mac-Donald Had a Farm," the knitting world reaps benefits, too. It's fun to experiment with these unusual fibers and fiber blends (often called "exotics"). Many of these exotic fibers come from very large animals that you would not want to meet in a dark alley. Some intrepid fiber lovers, however, figured out that even huge and scary-looking beasts have very soft fiber underneath one or more layers of coarse outer hair. It's this undercoat that is used to make hand-knitting yarns.

The most common exotics you'll encounter are yak and bison, both herd animals. Yaks are native to central Asia, where they have been used for centuries as pack animals and for their hair, milk, meat, and hides. Bison are native to the United States, where overhunting during the nineteenth and twentieth centuries reduced the population nearly to extinction. Bison numbers are increasing again, although they are still a fraction of what they were at the end of the nineteenth century. You may also have seen someone swoon at the mention of qiviut (pronounced KIV-ee-oot). The qiviut is a species of musk ox native to Alaska and northern parts of Canada. As with the bison and yak, fiber is gathered from the ox's undercoat, and because the population of qiviut is small, this fiber is relatively scarce, hence its high price. Occasionally, you'll encounter camel yarn; camels shed every year, and their fiber is gathered (or combed) to remove the outer guard hairs, then made into yarn.

The fibers from these large beasts share many characteristics: they are very warm but lightweight, they are good insulators when wet, they are durable, and they are extremely soft, often with a micron count comparable to cashmere. While these fibers don't have the amount of elasticity that wool does, they are not completely inelastic like, say, linen or cotton. These fibers do not shrink or felt like wool does and therefore are a bit easier to launder. They are hypoallergenic and breathable. Because of their price, and to create a more balanced yarn, these luxury fibers are often blended with other fibers, like wool (for a springier blend) or silk (to add shine). Many of these fibers don't bleach well, so you will see yarn in natural shades like brown and tan or muted colors created by overdyeing the natural colors. Their relative cost makes them more suitable for accessories rather than full garments for most knitters, but their beauty makes them well worth a try.

## ANGORA

Angora fiber is a very fluffy, very warm fiber derived from the Angora rabbit. Angora rabbits come in several breeds with varied traits and colors. Go to a county fair or fiber festival and, if you're lucky, you may see an Angora breeder sitting at her spinning wheel with a giant bunny on her lap, slowly and gently teasing out the rabbit's fibers and spinning them into yarn right on the spot. Angora fiber is plucked, combed, or shorn from the rabbit—the animals are not killed to harvest the fiber. The fiber itself is tremendously soft—and did I mention it's very warm? One reason angora is blended with other fibers or used only in small amounts as trim is because of this warmth. Angora is also a fragile fiber that felts easily, and its short fibers make it prone to shedding. It has a distinct halo and is generally quite inelastic.

## POSSUM

In addition to the more common sources of animal fiber, you will occasionally come across some new or unusual animal source for fiber. For example, some extremely gorgeous yarns from New Zealand are made with possum fur. Note that this kind of possum is not the kind we see scrambling across the road in the headlights of our car, but rather a marsupial species that was brought to New Zealand in the early nineteenth century. With no natural predators, the species became a serious threat to the environment. Hunting is necessary to protect the island and its inhabitants. Instead of wasting the fur, mills harvest the fiber and turn it into beautiful yarn. Possum fur is lightweight, soft, and warm, and tends to have a slight halo. It's also a very short fiber and is often blended with other fibers.

It's theoretically possible to spin yarn out of all kinds of fiber, and so you may encounter yarns that contain unusual or rare fibers. I myself have hand-dyed yarn that was spun with a small percentage of dog fiber—from the long-haired, white Samoyed breed. (The yarn doesn't smell like wet dog—it is beautiful, with warmth and a silky feel.) Learn what you can about the fiber's inherent traits and then experiment. A cowl or scarf is a relatively small project but may be the perfect item to showcase an unusual type of yarn.

## VEGETABLE: PLANT FIBERS

Unlike animal fibers, which are made of protein, plant fibers are derived from cellulose. Cellulose is an organic compound that is structurally and compositionally different from keratin. Under a microscope, a cotton fiber would look like a smooth ribbon with gentle twists. This different structure causes cellulose fibers to behave very differently from animal fibers in several important ways.

Earlier we saw how the overlapping scales (and in some cases, the hollow cores) of animal fibers keep the wearer warm by trapping air near the body. Plant fibers don't have these scales and, therefore, don't insulate the way animal fibers do. What plant fibers are good at is releasing heat from the body and cooling the wearer. Knitters who live in hot climates and those of us whose personal thermostat always runs warm love the way plant-derived yarns keep us comfortable.

Another benefit of scales: they build elasticity into the fiber. The spaces between the scales give the fiber room to stretch out and bounce back. With their flat, scaleless structure, plant fibers don't have this built-in elasticity. Certain stitch patterns, especially those that require a great deal of stitch manipulation, may look untidy when worked in 100 percent plant fiber due to this inelasticity. Inelasticity also means that your knitted garment may lose its original shape over time or grow in length as you wear it. You can re-block cellulose fibers, but over the years, you may find that it's harder and harder to get the yarn to return to its original shape. This inelasticity does, however, have the advantage of enhancing drape in many plant-derived fibers.

Plant fibers are very strong, and they don't felt, which is a great advantage if you need to wash your knitted items frequently. (Note that your items may shrink, at least temporarily, if they are left in the dryer too long.) Plant-based fibers don't attract moths (yay!), one very distinct advantage over animal fibers, but, unfortunately, they're not completely carefree, as they can be affected by mold or mildew. Plant fibers absorb water well, so make sure all items are completely dry before putting them away or in storage, to avoid discovering this very unpleasant surprise.

Other advantages to plant fibers: They're made from renewable resources and are not derived in any way from animals, factors that are important to some knitters. They do not trigger allergies and sensitivities the way animal fibers may. They also tend to be significantly cheaper than animal fibers, making them attractive to the budget-minded knitter.

Consider plant-derived fibers, then, when you're choosing a yarn for warm-weather items like tank tops, lightweight shawls, or knitted tees. Plant fibers are also popular for baby items since they are hypoallergenic and often machine washable (always check the label, of course!). Hardier fibers like linen and hemp are perfect for items that need to be durable, such as bags or washcloths. Think twice about using 100 percent plant fiber for very intricate stitch patterns that require a great deal of yarn manipulation. You'll also want to consider plant fiber's inherent tendency to drape and/or stretch, which is delightful for shawls and layering pieces, but less appealing for snug-fitting items or tailored garments that need to hold their shape.

## COTTON

Of all the plant fibers, cotton is the most popular. Cotton yarn begins as the fluffy white fiber that surrounds the seeds of the cotton plant. When cotton is picked, the seeds of the cotton are mixed in with this soft white fiber. A handy machine called the cotton gin, invented in 1794 (remember Eli Whitney from history class?), separates the fiber from the seeds. The fiber can then be cleaned and put into bales. Small samples are taken and used to grade the cotton, after which it's sent to mills and factories for spinning.

Cotton has many advantages when it comes to hand-knitting: it's soft, it's breathable, and it's hypoallergenic, for starters. Cotton also absorbs moisture, is strong, and is less expensive compared to many other fibers. It takes dye well, so you can find a multitude of colors (although keep an eye out for bleeding when you wash deep or bright colors). Cotton is biodegradable, too, although conventionally grown cotton tends to use significant amounts of pesticides.

Cotton fiber is probably best known for its cushy softness, making it perfect for next-to-skin wear. As with wool, certain strains of the cotton plant have been cultivated to maximize desirable qualities like fineness and softness, and yarn made from such varieties (see page 38) will have a particularly plush feel. How cotton is prepared also affects its softness and performance. If the cotton fibers are combed before spinning, which removes shorter and damaged fibers, the resulting yarn—called combed

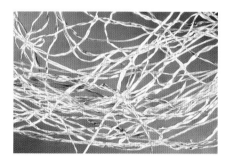

Individual cotton fibers resemble flat ribbons.

Microscopic view of cotton fibers

Cotton boll

cotton—will be even softer and finer than uncombed cotton. More loosely spun cotton yarns feel softer, too, although the looser the twist, the more likely the fiber is to show signs of wear (such as pilling).

In addition to inelasticity, one disadvantage to cotton is its relative heaviness. A 100-yard ball of cotton weighs more than a 100-yard ball of wool, for example. That makes cotton less suited for big projects or stitch patterns requiring the yarn to cross over itself (like cables). The combination of weight and inelasticity will result in noticeable sag. Knit a cabled sweater out of cotton and, in a few years, you'll have a maxi-dress! You'll also want to think about the structure of the yarn: singles yarns (or singles with a very thin binder) are more likely to pill and show wear, while twisted, chained, or cabled cottons are more durable, although they may feel slightly less soft. One last thing to keep in mind: If using a singles yarn made from cotton, be sure to see whether the yarn is so tightly twisted that it creates bias (see page 54). If a swatch knit in stockinette stitch skews to one side, you may need to switch to a different stitch pattern or play with blocking to eliminate or minimize the fabric's bias.

## COTTON LOVERS' LINGO

**Mercerized cotton** has been subjected to a special chemical process to make the yarn shinier, smoother, and stronger. Dye also adheres better to mercerized fibers, allowing for brighter and deeper colors. **Perle cotton** is a specific type of mercerized cotton.

**Pima cotton** is yarn made from a specific strain of cotton that produces longer, stronger fibers. The added fiber length results in a smoother, softer hand and increased durability. Supima® cotton is a brand name that is licensed for use only by pima cotton yarns that meet specific standards of quality. **Egyptian cotton** and **Sea Island cotton** are other strains of cotton renowned for their extra-long fibers. Longer, stronger fibers create a softer and more durable fabric. You will, of course, pay more for these, just as you would pay more for 100 percent merino wool.

**Organic cotton** has become increasingly popular, although the term *organic* can mean many things. The goal is to grow and process the cotton in a way that has less impact on the environment. Producers use non-genetically modified plants, for example, and avoid synthetic pesticides, defoliants, and other chemicals. Proponents of organic cotton tout the reduction or elimination of chemicals and pesticides compared to conventionally grown cotton, leading to less pollution, better-quality soils, and improved biodiversity. Organic cotton does tend to cost more than conventionally grown fiber. While the label "organic" is frequently used, that label doesn't necessarily guarantee the manufacturer is certified as organic and complies with the USDA National Organic Program standards.

## LINEN

Humans have been making linen yarn and fabric for thousands of years—even though it's neither an easy nor a fast process. Linen yarn is made from the flax plant, a tall annual with blue flowers that is relatively easy to grow. Linen is harvested either by pulling the plant out of the ground, roots and all, or by cutting it close to the root so that the fiber itself stays as long as possible. The stalks are cleaned, dried, and deseeded, then soaked until the substance that holds the fibers together (called lignin) decomposes. The usable fiber is found in the inner section of the plant, so the outer and inner layers must be mechanically separated, then combed to remove any short fibers. Only afterward can the linen fiber be spun into yarn. Finer fibers are spun while wet to minimize breakage (you'll often see "wet spun" on the yarn label), although shorter fibers are often spun while dry. Because processing linen is such a time-consuming and multistep process, good-quality linen is more expensive than many other fabrics.

Flowering flax

The result of all this processing is a yarn noted for its strength and durability as well as its beauty. Linen is one of the strongest natural fibers available and lasts a very long time—it's so strong, it's added to paper money to improve its durability. It's cool to wear and hypoallergenic. Like all plant fibers, linen is known for its inelasticity—it has no spring or bounce, and many knitters find that working with it causes hand strain. Linen's natural inelasticity, however, means that it drapes beautifully. Another plus: linen softens markedly with wear, use, and laundering.

As with cotton, you'll want to use linen for warm-weather wear, focusing on patterns where drape is an important design element. Linen is also well suited to projects that take advantage of its strength and durability, such as market bags or washcloths. Linen does well as part of a yarn blend, adding coolness and drape. Just as plant fibers react to dye differently than animal fibers, linen blends may take on a heathered look or can develop extra complexity as different types of dyes are used, each adhering to one type of fiber.

A handful of other plant fibers can be made into yarn, and they behave very similarly to linen. Nettle yarn (also called aloo) is derived from the stinging nettle plant and has a long history of use in Nepal. Hemp yarn is derived from the cannabis plant (made from varieties with a higher proportion of fiber) and has been cultivated for nonrecreational use for hundreds of years.

## EXTRUDED FIBERS

Have you ever made fresh spaghetti with an old-fashioned pasta maker? You load dough into the pasta maker, attach the metal blade that will create the shape you want, then turn the handle and crank out your linguine or spaghetti. An entire class of yarns, called extruded yarn, is made using a similar process. Because extruded yarns are most often made from cellulose fiber, I've included them in this section.

To make an extruded yarn, the source material (often bamboo or wood pulp) is heated, crushed, or added to a solvent or other chemical agent, turning it into a viscous semiliquid. Once the material takes this thick liquid or gel-like form, it is pressed through a spinnerette, a metal cap or nozzle with small holes. The manufacturer can use spinnerettes with different-shaped holes to create different-shaped yarns. After extrusion, the yarn is allowed to dry or solidify. Dye can be either added to the mix before extrusion or applied to the finished yarn in the traditional manner.

The chart opposite lists many common plant-based sources for extruded yarns, like wood pulp, as well as some newer sources like sugar beets and milk protein.

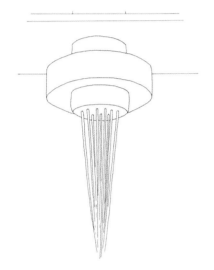

Fiber extruder

| YARN | SOURCE | QUALITIES |
|------|--------|-----------|
| RAYON | Wood and/or paper pulp | Takes dye especially well |
| VISCOSE | Same as rayon | Type of rayon made via different process |
| MODAL | Wood pulp from beech trees | Type of rayon; processing is more eco-friendly |
| TENCEL® OR LYOCELL | Same as rayon | Type of rayon; processing is more eco-friendly |
| BAMBOO | Bamboo plants | Reputed to have antibacterial qualities; particularly soft and silky; pest-resistant |
| SOY | Leftover proteins from soybean processing | Drapes very well |
| CORN | Starches in corn | May come from GMO corn; may melt if exposed to high heat |
| SUGARCANE | Leftover plant material from sugar processing | Has drape and sheen |
| SEAWEED | Seaweed fiber added to lyocell | Reputed to have anti-inflammatory effect; trace elements from seaweed reputed to enhance skin of knitter |
| MILK | Casein (milk protein) | Reputed to have antibacterial and antifungal qualities |

While extruded yarns can behave in different ways depending on their shape, they tend to share the following characteristics:

- They are extremely soft and good for next-to-skin wear.
- They are breathable and comfortable to wear (assuming they are made of plant-based fibers).
- They take dye well.
- They are relatively inelastic but have wonderful drape.
- They often have a rich luster.

Synthetic fibers can also be extruded, but be sure you don't confuse the method of processing with the source fiber. Sometimes all extruded fibers are incorrectly considered "synthetic." Make sure to check the fiber content to know for sure. If the raw ingredients for these yarns are entirely plant derived, then the resulting yarns are made of natural fibers (and will have the breathability and other qualities of cellulose fibers). In the United States, federal regulations require extruded yarns to be labeled "rayon" (whether or not they are actually made from wood pulp like true rayon); some manufacturers use the designation "rayon from bamboo" (or whatever the original fiber source is) so that consumers understand exactly where the fiber came from. Whether a specific yarn is good or bad for the environment is an entirely different issue and does not depend solely on whether it's a "natural" or "synthetic" fiber. Some believe that using biodegradable and sustainable fibers like bamboo is an improvement over synthetic yarns made from petrochemicals, but others believe that the benefits of using plant fibers are offset by chemical use and other environmental effects of processing. I'll let you decide for yourself.

## Animal + Vegetable = Silk?

Silk, that gorgeous, soft, lustrous fiber, doesn't neatly fall into the animal or the vegetable categories. Silk comes from silkworms, which are animals (sort of), and it's made of proteins, so in that sense it could be considered an animal fiber. On the other hand, silk does not have scales the way other animal fibers do and is made from the leaves that silkworms eat in copious amounts. For simplicity's sake, I've given silk its own section.

If you want to cultivate silk, then you've got to start with bugs. While many insects secrete silky fiber, most commercial silk comes from the Bombyx silkworm (*Bombyx mori*). Silkworms are the larval stage of the Bombyx moth. Female silk moths can lay large numbers of eggs in a short period of time (which is a good thing, since they have a very brief lifespan, about four to five days). The eggs hatch, producing caterpillars (or larvae). Like any other caterpillar, silk larvae eat voraciously—until they are approximately ten thousand times heavier than when they hatched. The Bombyx silkworm eats only mulberry leaves, which is why silk fabric is sometimes described as "mulberry silk."

When the caterpillars are ready to spin their cocoons, they begin to excrete a special fluid from two openings near their jaws (called spinnerets,

*Bombyx mori:* the silkworm

just like the nozzle used for extruded fibers). This fluid consists of a protein called fibroin, along with a second, gummy protein called sericin, which allows the two strands (one from each spinneret) to stick together. The silk fiber hardens when it hits the air. The silkworm continually excretes this fiber, wrapping it around and around itself to form a protective cocoon. Typically, the silkworm finishes its cocoon in two to three days, creating as much as 1,000 or more yards of extremely fine thread—thread a fraction of the width of a human hair in diameter.

To harvest this fine silk fiber requires exact timing. If the farmer waits too long, the caterpillar will turn into a moth, destroying its cocoon as it emerges. Once the moth breaks up the long silk strands, the remaining fibers are too short to unwind. When the time is right, the sericulturist immerses the cocoon in boiling water to kill the pupa (some sericulturists use steam or hot air for this part of the process) and to loosen the silk fibers that are wound and stuck together in the cocoon. The sericulturist can then unwind the unbroken strands of silk and combine them into thread. The silk thread is cleaned and spun into yarn. Any broken bits of silk and the short ends of the fiber aren't wasted; the precious silk is washed to remove remaining sericin and combed to align the fibers. It can then be processed into yarn known as "raw silk," which has a nubby, less shiny finish than regular silk.

It's no secret that one of silk's best qualities is its hand: incredibly soft, smooth, and luxurious. If you looked at silk fibers under a microscope, you'd see that they have a smooth, slightly triangular shape. This shape creates many angles that reflect light, giving the fiber remarkable shine and luster. Because it doesn't have interlocking scales like most protein fibers, but has a smooth surface, silk is a very fluid fabric. It has excellent drape and an overall flowing, floating quality. Silk also dyes especially well, and this trait, when combined with its natural sheen, makes for lovely rich and saturated colors. Silk fibers are very strong (silk was used for parachutes in World War II), although different types of yarn construction have varying levels of durability. Silk also insulates well and wicks moisture away from the body, so silk underwear is more functional than it may seem.

If silk has any downside, it would be its inelasticity (as we've seen before, no scales means no stretching and bouncing back), which can make silk garments sag out of shape and can be tough on a knitter's hands. Silk may pill if it is softly spun and if its fibers are close to the surface of the fabric. Some knitters find silk to be slippery on the needles, although using wooden or bamboo needles can help slow down those stitches. Silk also requires special care when it comes to washing. It must be treated very gently to avoid fiber damage. Many of these disadvantages can be offset by using silk blends. For example, blending wool with silk helps add elasticity and memory, while still allowing for super softness and shine.

## "MINERAL" FIBERS

While there are fibers that are actually made from minerals, like asbestos, it's doubtful that you'd ever knit with them. Instead, I use the "mineral" category as a catchall for yarns made of things other than animal (protein) or plant (cellulose) fibers.

## SYNTHETIC YARNS

I sometimes say that knitters can argue about anything, and if you don't believe me, then ask your knitting group what they think about synthetic yarns. I have always preferred natural fibers in my clothing and yarn, but I have come to appreciate the many things synthetic fibers bring to the table. Synthetic fibers are inexpensive, which means more yarn (and therefore more knitting) for people on tight budgets or who like big projects (like yarn-bombing a bridge). Synthetic fibers are very easy to launder, going through washer and dryer without mishap. Synthetic yarns are very durable (when the world ends, the cockroaches that remain will cuddle up under acrylic blankets as they survey their domain). Synthetic fibers are resistant to mold and mildew, impervious to moths, and hypoallergenic. They can be made in many styles and shapes, tend to be soft, and don't shrink or sag.

Like every other fiber, synthetic yarns have their downsides. They don't breathe like natural fibers do, and thus they can be very hot to wear and feel clammy when wet. Synthetic yarns are not biodegradable and are made from nonrenewable, petroleum-based sources. Although durable, they pill fairly readily and are prone to static cling. They are challenging to block: some say it is impossible to block synthetic yarns because they eventually spring back to their original shape, but others find that using steam *very carefully* can affect a kind of blocking. Which brings us to another downside of synthetic yarns: they do not react well to direct heat. If you are close to a heat source or put a hot iron directly on the yarn, it may melt and cause burns to your skin or emit fumes that could make you ill.

## KILLING THE FIBER

No, it's not a knitting horror story; the phrase "killing the fiber" refers to the process of applying too much steam or heat to a yarn, particularly synthetic yarns, so that the yarn loses its body and gets saggy and droopy. Occasionally a designer will use the process deliberately, to create a garment with extra drape, but when applying steam or heat to a yarn, especially synthetic ones, be careful you don't kill it.

Regardless of their faults, synthetic yarns are very useful. If you knit premie baby caps for your local hospital, you really must use acrylic yarn so that the caps can stand up to the challenges of institutional laundering as well as to avoid allergic reactions on tender skin. If you need easy-care knitting that cannot be ruined in the wash, whether for a tot or a college student, synthetic yarns just can't be beat. If you haven't knit with synthetic yarn in a while, you may be surprised at the improvements made in recent years. Textile manufacturers have figured out how to create extremely fine synthetic fibers, with diameters smaller than that of human hair or even silk. These microfibers, as they are called, feel more like natural fibers, are lighter weight than traditional synthetics, and are better at "breathing" than many traditional synthetics. Look for these synthetics at your local yarn shop.

Here again, I'll stand up for yarn blends as giving the knitter the best of multiple worlds. Adding synthetic fiber to cotton lightens the resulting blend, for example, and helps the garment keep its shape significantly better than cotton alone. Adding polyamide to wool sock yarn adds durability, especially for heels and toes, which get the most wear. Elastic gives real stretch to cotton fibers, making hand-knit cotton socks practical. Nylon can help hold a mix of fibers together, especially where the fibers are of different lengths. Adding less expensive synthetics to a yarn blend can make the skein more affordable while maintaining a relatively high percentage of natural fiber. Thus it's best to judge each synthetic fiber and each synthetic-containing yarn on their own terms, as they can be quite useful. This cheat sheet will help you compare some of the most common types of synthetic yarn.

| FIBER | DESCRIPTION | DETAILS |
|---|---|---|
| NYLON (POLYAMIDE) | Originally created as a potential substitute for silk | Very durable; holds its shape; good for holding a blend of different fibers together |
| POLYESTER | May appear under the brands Dacron® and Coolmax® | Wrinkle-resistant; holds its shape; strong |
| ACRYLIC | Good all-purpose synthetic; made in filaments then spun into yarn as wool is | Dyes well; often blended with other fibers |
| POLYPROPYLENE | Great at wicking moisture away | Very lightweight |
| ELASTIC | Incorporates woven strips of rubber to allow it to spring back to its original shape | Extremely stretchy |

## UNUSUAL FIBER SOURCES

As manufacturers and artisans experiment, you may encounter yarns made from new or unusual fiber sources. Some are functional and others are used for artistic or political purposes. In recent years, I've heard of raffia yarn (a sturdy and somewhat stiff plant-based fiber), banana yarn (using fiber from banana tree leaves), and paper yarn (a favorite in Japan). A few manufacturers make yarn with stainless steel in it, creating a unique and moldable fiber that can be used for jewelry or for items intended to hold their shapes. Fiber artists often seek out materials to recycle into knitting, such as plastic garbage bags, old T-shirts, or even the "guts" of cassette tapes. Yarns made of these unusual fibers must be judged based on their own unique qualities, and often have limited practical application for the typical knitter.

## FIBER FAVES

It's time to revisit your yarn lists—this time to look for insights about fiber content. You may notice some preferences right off the bat—a love for llama, or Bluefaced Leicester bliss—but think about how pleased you were with the finished project as well as how much you enjoyed handling the yarn. I once knit a baby sweater with a colorful intarsia motif on the front, using a machine-washable cotton yarn. When I was done, I realized the sweater looked a little off; the smooth cotton didn't mesh together where the colors changed, leaving holes. In that case, I liked knitting with the yarn just fine but wasn't pleased with the result because smooth cotton yarn wasn't the best choice for colorwork. Now that you have a better understanding of how different fibers act on the needles, you may decide it wasn't the yarn you disliked, it was the combination of yarn and pattern.

# 3

# YARN CONSTRUCTION: SINGLES, PLIES, AND MORE

While fiber content plays an important role in determining how a yarn will behave, yarn construction—how the yarn is built—is equally important. Think about water, made up of two hydrogen atoms and one oxygen atom. All water is made of those ingredients, in those proportions. But think how differently water behaves depending on the form it takes. Ice cubes are solid and hard; liquid water is pourable and drinkable; fog blocks our vision even though a hand can slide right through it. Yet all of them are made of the same stuff.

Yarn is the same way. While different types of fiber have inherent qualities that cannot be changed, those inherent qualities can be amplified or downplayed based on the way the yarn is prepared. So let's take a closer look at the various ways fiber can be turned into yarn, paying close attention to the effect that yarn construction has on the way the yarn behaves on the needles.

## SPUN YARNS

The traditional way to turn fiber into yarn is to spin it. To spin yarn, all you need is clean, loose fiber and a way to add twist. Twist is the most important ingredient when spinning yarn, because twist adds the energy that transforms loose fiber into strands strong enough to knit. You can add twist mechanically—by industrial machine or foot-powered wheel, or with a flick of your wrist on a spindle. You can even spin yarn with your bare hands, by taking some loose fiber and rubbing it in one direction in your palms until it forms a strand of yarn. Adding a small amount of twist—rubbing it only a little—will create something resembling a strand, but the strand won't be very strong; you may be able to pull it apart with a gentle tug. Too much twist—lots and lots of rubbing—and the strand will be tight, almost twitching with built-up energy. The tightly twisted strand of yarn won't be as soft to the touch, either, although it will be much stronger than the loosely spun strand. Somewhere in the middle of these two extremes is yarn with the perfect amount of twist.

Many variables go into the spinning process, including the type of fiber used, how the fiber is prepared, and how many plies make up the yarn. We've already looked at the characteristics of different fibers. Now let's talk about fiber preparation.

## FIBER PREPARATION: WOOLEN VS. WORSTED YARNS

Anyone who has ever made yarn will tell you that preparing the fiber before you spin is a crucial part of the process. Raw fiber for spinning is made of thousands of loose, individual filaments. As the fiber is gathered and processed, those individual filaments lie in different directions, like a set of pick-up sticks that have been dumped on the floor. Instead of trying to spin this jumble of fiber, mills card the fiber first.

Fiber can be carded by running it through a machine or using a hand-held tool that has rows of tiny metal pins. Carding removes impurities, like dried vegetable matter, and helps pull out short or damaged fibers. It can also be used to mix together different batches of fiber. The result is a kind of webbing or airy sheet. Some fiber goes through an additional process called combing. Combing is just what it sounds like: metal teeth pass through the fiber to straighten and align the individual filaments. Combing also removes any remaining impurities and short or damaged fibers. Yarns that are carded only are called woolen (or woolen-spun) yarns; yarns that are both carded and combed are called worsted (or worsted-spun) yarns.*

---

\* The term *worsted* can mean different things in the world of fiber. Certain categories of yarns are called worsted-weight yarns, and there is a particular spinning technique called worsted-style spinning. In this section, we're using worsted's third definition to refer to yarns that are spun after both carding *and* combing the fiber.

Because the fiber is prepared differently, woolen and worsted yarns are very different creatures.

Woolen yarns (i.e., carded only) are spun from fiber that has filaments that are not perfectly aligned but retain a somewhat haphazard nature, leaving room in the spaces between the filaments to trap air. Worsted-spun yarns, on the other hand, have filaments that line up parallel to each other. These parallel fibers are compact and have no room for air in between them. (Imagine lining up the pick-up sticks so they are parallel, forming a compact mass as you slip them in the can.)

What does this mean for you, the knitter? Even before you cast on your first stitch, you'll notice a difference in the appearance of the yarns. Woolen yarns, with their jumbled fibers, tend to look fuzzier and more rustic than worsted yarns. Worsted yarns, on the other hand, have a neater and crisper look, with their lined-up fibers and smoother finish. If you look closely, even the individual fibers in the yarns present differently, with the individual fibers of a woolen yarn more distinct in a kind of controlled chaos, while the fibers in a worsted spun are very orderly and unobtrusive, blending neatly into the whole.

When it comes to knitting with these yarns, the differences are even more pronounced. The air trapped inside woolen yarns insulates and makes these yarns warmer. It also gives them a lofty, squishy feel. On the other hand, the compactness of worsted yarns makes them denser and heavier. They don't insulate as well because they lack the air pockets and therefore aren't quite as warm as their woolen cousins.

Another important difference is gauge. Again, the air trapped inside woolen-spun yarns is key: it gives them more versatility when it comes to gauge. The trapped air leaves room for the individual fibers to compress or expand as the yarn is knit. That means woolen yarns can be knit at a wider variety of gauges. A smaller needle size will give a tighter gauge and a denser fabric, while bigger needles give a looser gauge and a more pliable fabric. When knit at a typical gauge, a woolen yarn is likely to bloom after blocking, again because of the space in between the fibers. Worsted-spun yarns have less flexibility when it comes to gauge because they are denser, and individual fibers have less room to move.

The fact that the fibers of woolen yarns are often shorter and jumbled affects how these yarns perform. Shorter fibers are harder to control and may stick out more, plus their less orderly arrangement in the strand creates a fuzzier, hairier finish. (This fuzzier finish, with fiber ends sticking out, may explain why particularly sensitive folks find woolen yarns a little itchy when worn next to the skin.) Stitch definition may also suffer a bit with woolen-spun yarns, due to the fuzzier finish, whereas worsted-spun yarns tend to have clear and distinct stitch definition. Finally, woolen yarns aren't as strong as worsted ones. If you tug too hard on a woolen-spun strand, it may break or pull apart as the fibers separate. If you're a fan of stranded color knitting, however, you probably adore woolen-spun yarns because the fibers will mesh together and create a cohesive fabric that makes the gaps between yarns less apparent and holds floats in place.

Worsted-spun yarns have many advantages, too. With fibers combed so they line up in one direction, the resulting yarn will feel smooth and silky, instead of fuzzy. This smoothness means that worsted yarns have crisper stitch definition, without loose strands that create a halo. A slipperier finish also means that worsted yarns drape better. Without air trapped between fibers, worsted yarns tend to insulate less effectively and aren't quite as warm as woolen yarns, although their relative density makes

This woolen yarn is perfect for colorwork.

them resistant to wind and rain. Worsted yarns may feel softer without the fuzzy structure of their cousins, and they are significantly stronger—you'll have a hard time trying to pull the yarn apart!

When considering a substitution, find out if the original yarn is worsted or woolen spun. If it's woolen spun, determine whether the designer is knitting the yarn at the expected gauge or whether the gauge may be looser or tighter than is typical (see page 83). If you pick a worsted-spun yarn to substitute for the woolen, make sure to swatch it carefully, as the worsted-spun yarn will not have as much room to expand or contract to match gauge. Woolen-spun yarns are excellent for warm sweaters and hats, for Fair Isle and other stranded projects, for outerwear, and for lace (the slight stickiness of the yarn will hold the pattern together, while the loftiness means it will block well). Worsted-spun yarns are great for projects that require more drape and that involve texture or other stitchwork that benefits from good stitch definition. They are good for close-to-the-skin wear and, because they are sturdier, are good for projects that will be subjected to abrasion, such as socks.

Now that we've got fiber preparation out of the way, let's look at how yarns are built.

This worsted-spun yarn has terrific stitch definition.

## "SINGLES" YARNS

Once the fiber is prepared, it's time to spin some yarn. The starting point for building a yarn is creating one strand of twisted fiber. When knitted by itself, it is called a "singles" yarn. Many beloved yarns are singles, including Noro Kureyon, Malabrigo Worsted, Manos del Uruguay Maxima, and Cascade Yarns® Spuntaneous, to name but a few.

Singles yarns have many wonderful qualities. Without any other strands wrapped tightly around it, the individual filaments in the fiber have room to move, with air inside. This gives singles yarns softness and loft. The fact that singles are not tightly twisted or wrapped around another ply also means that the individual characteristics of the fiber can show through: the gloss of silk, the subtle color variations in multifiber blends, and so on. After blocking, singles yarns often bloom, creating a more relaxed fabric.

This singles yarn is lofty and soft.

At the same time, singles yarns have their disadvantages. The trade-off for a singles yarn's softness is that it is more likely to show wear and abrasion as it's worn. The individual fibers of the yarn are close to the surface and are only held together by a minimal amount of twist. That means that even a little bit of friction can cause the individual fibers to pull out of the yarn and form pills. (You'll notice pilling and other damage wherever your garment tends to rub against other surfaces, like at the elbows, cuffs, and hems.)

This loose twist has other repercussions on your knitting. If you tug on the yarn or need to manipulate stitches with some force, you may find that singles yarns pull apart as you knit with them—irksome when you're in the middle of a project or working a complex stitch pattern. Sometimes singles split as you're knitting, causing your needle to slip through the middle of the strand instead of around it. This may make your knitting look sloppy when sections of a strand aren't pulled cleanly through the loops. Needles with blunter tips and/or a smooth coating (I like Addi Turbo® needles) can help minimize splitting.

Sometimes singles can be twisted a bit too loosely or tightly. Spun too loosely, singles will not hold their shape and will break and pull apart. Yet singles with too much twist can also be problematic. Whether deliberate (as when a hand-spinner creates what are called energized singles) or unintentional (as when a new spinner adds too much twist), overtwisted yarns will feel hard and may torque or kink back on themselves as you are working with them.

Another common issue with singles, especially those with lots of twist, is biasing. Biasing occurs when the twist in a yarn goes in only one direction. Individual stitches lean in the direction of the twist, pulling the knitted fabric to that side. Instead of looking like a rectangle with right angles for corners, your swatch will look more like a parallelogram. Blocking can help minimize the tendency of some yarns to bias, but because the problem lies in the structure of the yarn itself, you won't always be able to block bias out. Using a stitch pattern with texture and one that has a roughly equal distribution of knits and purls is likely to give you a less biased fabric, but again, this may only minimize rather than eliminate the problem. You'll have to swatch to be sure whether and how much an overtwisted yarn will bias, but if you find yourself stopping in the middle of your knitting to let the skein dangle down and untwist, keep an eye out for bias in the fabric.

## PLIED YARNS

Most yarns are categorized as plied yarns, as they are made up of two or more strands twisted around each other. (Each constituent strand of a

Bias occurs when stitches lean into the direction of the twist.

multistrand yarn is called a ply.) You've probably heard yarns described as "2-ply" or "4-ply," depending on how many constituent strands they have. (Note that if you call a singles yarn a "single ply," you may be corrected by a spinner. Technically, a ply refers to one strand of many; because there are not multiple strands of yarn in singles yarns, they reason, the term *one-ply* is an oxymoron.) Yarns can be constructed by combining any number of plies, although 2-ply, 3-ply, and 4-ply yarns are the most common.

A plied yarn features multiple strands twisted around each other.

Most commercial yarns are plied yarns instead of singles yarns. Why? Leaving aside yarn purists, who insist that "real yarn" must have two or more plies (eye roll), plied yarns do have certain advantages over singles that make them more appealing to the typical knitter. The most significant are balance and stability.

We saw earlier how single yarns are held together by a twist that runs in one direction only. Add a second strand with twist running in the opposite direction, however, and everything changes. Each ply has another ply to lean on, with energy headed in a different direction. Instead of leaning to one side, the different twists balance each other out so your knitted fabric won't bias (thus you may hear yarns with both clockwise and counterclockwise twist described as "balanced").

Plied yarn is also stronger than singles yarn. Each ply adds more strength to the mix, while the wrapped structure of the yarn makes it more durable. Each ply holds in the individual fibers and locks them tight, making them less likely to pill or abrade. If you're a spinner, you may have noticed how plying evens out the surface of inconsistencies in yarn, camouflaging slightly thicker or thinner areas.

Two-ply yarns tend to have a slightly bumpy texture because of the way the plies curve around each other, which is sometimes described as a "string of pearls" texture. Yarns with three plies tend to have a smoother surface with each of the three plies spiraling around a hollow core. Spinning expert Abby Franquemont notes that 2-ply yarns tend to feel "grabby" as the bumps from each strand intersect, while yarns with three or more plies are slipperier and have more drape. The strands in a 2-ply yarn have room to move and therefore are good for lace knitting and other stitches that require a stern blocking. Yarns with additional plies are denser, and thus are ideal for items like socks or mittens intended to keep the wearer warm.

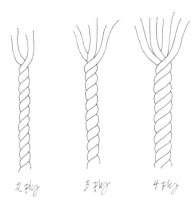

2 ply    3 ply    4 ply

## PLY-ON-PLY YARNS

If you take two singles and ply them together, you get a 2-ply yarn. If you take two or more plied yarns and ply them together, you get an entirely new creature. In creating some of these ply-on-ply yarns, as I've dubbed them, the precise method of spinning comes into play. Yarns can be twisted in either a clockwise direction or a counterclockwise direction called Z twist and S twist, respectively. When building ply-on-ply yarns, the direction of the twist is significant.

Cabled yarns, for example, are made by combining two single yarns spun clockwise, then plied counterclockwise; a second yarn is created the same way, and both 2-plies are then plied together clockwise. Cabled yarns are very strong and stable, because they are so balanced—plies twisted in one direction are balanced by plies spun in the opposite direction. Cabled yarns also tend to have good stitch definition and a crisp finish. You may be familiar with Tahki Cotton Classic, a cabled yarn with the characteristic strength, stitch definition, and the ropelike appearance of this category of yarns.

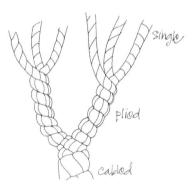

If all plies are twisted in the same direction, the yarn is called a multistrand yarn. Multistrand yarns tend to have smooth finishes and good stitch definition. As the brilliant Clara Parkes points out, knitting with a multistrand yarn produces a very characteristic effect in the fabric: "In simple stockinette, the left legs of the stitches tend to stack on top of one another, resulting in a faint vertical stripe up the fabric." This effect is produced by the shared direction of the individual plies.

For yarn substitution purposes, what's important to remember is that ply-on-ply yarns are strong, balanced, and durable, and have excellent stitch definition. If you are interested in learning more about directional twist and yarns with layers of ply, consult one of the spinning references (see pages 165 and 166).

## UNTRADITIONAL SPUN YARNS

Most spun yarns are spun smoothly and consistently, with an eye to producing a yarn of uniform thickness. Play around with the spinning process, however, and hilarity (or at least an interesting yarn) ensues.

Thick-and-thin yarns like the one above have (as the name implies) strands of varying width. Some sections of the yarn are very thick, while other sections are very thin (sometimes threadlike), so that the width of the strand constantly varies. (You may also hear the term *slub* used to describe yarns that have variations in texture along the strand, whether thicker areas or knots interspersed at regular or irregular intervals.) Thick-and-thin yarns can create some very interesting textural effects but can produce an uneven fabric with inconsistent gauge. They tend to be singles yarns, which make them less durable, as do the inconsistencies in thickness, making them good for garments that get light wear, like shawls, scarves, and cowls. Swatch carefully if you plan to try a more complicated stitch pattern. You may find that the thin or relatively unspun sections break when subjected to a lot of manipulation, while the thicker parts make maneuvers like knitting two stitches together awkward.

Bouclé yarns have little loops spaced along the strand of yarn. They are made by combining two yarns with different amounts of twist in them. The strand with more twist will kink up and double over the second strand, creating the loops. Depending on the exact spinning technique used, some bouclés have very obvious round loops along the strand, while in others, the yarn kinks in on itself and makes thick, bumpier loops. While bouclés have a soft, teddy-bear feel, they can be tricky to knit with. The loops make it very difficult to see the individual stitches, so it's tough to fix mistakes. Many knitters find that their needle tips get caught in the loops of a bouclé, making even simple stitches frustrating. It's best to use garter or stockinette stitch with bouclés, as more complex stitch patterns won't be visible, and make sure to take your time as you maneuver strands with loops and extra thickness. Bouclés have a soft feel and are great for adding texture to a project, so keep the stitches and shaping simple and enjoy the cushy feel of the fabric.

Tweed yarns, invariably associated with Scotland, Ireland, and other parts north, are rustic wools with flecks of multicolored fiber spun into the yarn. The flecks may be remnants from processing, they may be different types of fiber that take a different type of dye than the base yarn, or they may be deliberately dyed to create contrast. These flecks are sometimes called nepps or burrs. It's often said that the first tweed yarn was created accidentally but was so well received that it became a standard. Historically, tweeds have been made from wool that is spun woolen-style, although less traditional-looking tweeds, spun worsted or made of nonwool fibers or blends, are appearing on the market more frequently.

For yarn substitution purposes, remember that the way a tweed yarn is spun—worsted or woolen—will affect the way it behaves. Consider the visual effect of the nepps, too. Dyed in brighter colors, the nepps will stand out and capture the eye; if the nepps are dyed in more muted colors, they will have a subtler effect. Some knitters find that nepps get caught in the stitches and interfere with the movement of the needle, affecting gauge and stitch consistency; others do not notice a problem. Tweed yarns seem to fit especially well with cabled and other textural styles.

## WOVEN AND KNITTED YARNS

One alternative to plying yarns is to take spun thread or yarn and knit or weave it into a tube or ribbon. In the past, woven and knitted yarns were usually metallic or nylon ribbons and tapes, but now more traditional fibers like wool, alpaca, and linen are available in ribbon or tube form.

Ribbon and tape yarns are exactly as they sound—flat woven or knitted strands that look like ribbon or cloth tape. Many of these yarns are made with finished edges, although you may see tapes that are created by scoring fabric (note the unfinished edges which may curl or fray). Ribbon yarns often have metallic or glossy finishes, unusual textures, or interesting color effects; warm-weather fibers, like cotton and linen, are frequently made into tapes. Either way, a tape's or ribbon's structure can be tricky to work with. Tapes frequently twist when you work with them, and the yarn's flat shape may resist when you pull it through the loops of your stitches. Even after knitting, tape yarns may lie at a right angle to other stitches. That means that the overall look of the knitted fabric isn't always even or symmetric and your gauge may be uneven. You may also find that your needle's point gets snagged on the ribbon or tape; using blunt needle tips may help.

Tape yarn strand and swatch

Ribbon and tape yarns are wonderful for accent pieces like belts, scarves, or cowls. The yarn is not always sturdy (depending on fiber content), so high-wear items are not a good choice. Ribbon or tape yarns may also feel heavy in a larger garment, so use them judiciously, taking into account the potential for a heavy feel and the resulting stretch. They will have drape, especially if the surface is smooth and slippery.

Chainette yarns have become a popular alternative to woven or plied yarns. Chainette yarn is essentially an I-cord, a knitted tube with a hollow center. Sometimes the yarn is pressed into a flatter tape shape, while other times it remains more rounded. The name "chainette" refers to the surface of the yarn; its interlocking loops resemble chain mail or a chain-link fence. Chainette yarns have certain qualities that make them a valuable addition to the world of yarns. They can be knit from fibers with short filaments, such as cashmere, adding strength. They are lofty, with a squishy feel. Their hollow center makes them good insulators. They tend to have great stitch definition. Where chainette yarns really excel, however, is by adding a significant amount of elasticity even to fibers that aren't inherently elastic. If

Chainette yarn

you love an inelastic fiber but grow impatient with saggy sweaters or sore hands, find a chainette version to open up whole new worlds.

Remember that chainettes aren't as durable as tightly plied yarns; instead of strands that twist around each other, chainette yarns have a surface made up of knitted fabric. This means that they are prone to pilling and are not the best choice for items that will get hard wear. They also can be tricky to knit, at least until you get used to them; all of the teeny holes in between the stitches of the yarn are lying in wait to trap your needle!

You may encounter yarns that take the chainette construction one step further. Sometimes called Soffili® yarns, these yarns start with a knit tube, and then fill the inside of the tube with soft fiber. Because the outer knit tube holds the fibers inside, even unspun fiber can be used to fill the center. Soffili yarns have a plush texture and are warm. They also lend themselves to some fascinating color effects, since the manufacturer can vary the color, opacity, and/or fiber type of the inside filling and the outside tube of the yarn.

Soffili-style yarn

## EXTRUDED YARNS

We've already discussed a third way that yarns can be made. Extruded yarns are not spun, woven, or knit, but are created by first producing a gel-like mix of fiber and other substances, then pushing it through a nozzle. For more information about extruded yarns, see the discussion on page 40.

## NOVELTY YARNS

Thanks to the fantastic creativity of yarn manufacturers and spinners, there is a whole world of unique yarns that don't fall neatly into the above categories. These yarns often get lumped together in the "novelty yarn" category but can look strikingly different from each other. Their dramatic effects are created by unique constructions, combining different plies and textures, adding metallic accents, and mixing fibers. Keep in mind that it can be difficult to substitute a novelty yarn because of its uniqueness. While there are times when multiple companies produce very similar yarns, often there simply is no substitute for a unique and eye-catching novelty yarn. The photo below shows some common types of novelty yarn.

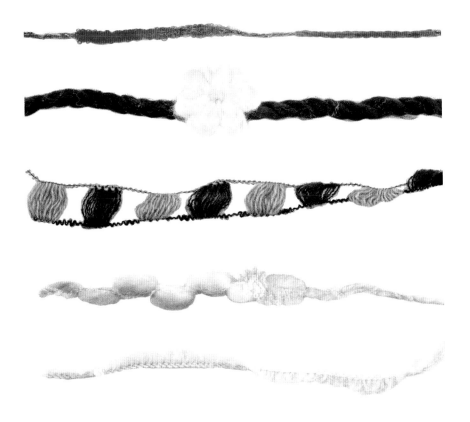

## EYELASH YARN (FAUX FUR)

When someone mentions novelty yarn, the first thing I think of is eyelash yarn. There was a time when eyelash yarn was all the rage, used for mitten and hat cuffs, scarves, cowls, and just about everything else you could imagine. Eyelash yarn is named for its structure: one main strand, usually

a

b

fairly thin, with long, colored fibers that stick out along the main strand and simulate the look of a false eyelash—or maybe a shag rug (a). Some eyelash yarn is colored to look like real fur, while other kinds use bright colors, metallic fiber, or interesting color combinations to create wilder effects.

As with all highly textured yarns, eyelash yarn can be tricky to knit. You may need to stop and slip out the individual "lashes" and fluff them with your fingers if they get trapped in the loops of stitches. The longer the lashes, the harder it is to see individual stitches, and the overall shaggy effect will cover up most stitch patterns. Eyelash yarns can have a heavy feel, too, which may affect their practicality for sweaters and other large garments. They are nearly always made of synthetic fiber.

## CHENILLE

Chenille is one of those love-it-or-hate-it yarns. It tends to take a flat, tapelike form, with small tufts of fiber cropped short and fastened closely together across a central strand (b). A strand of chenille yarn looks like a pipe cleaner—or one of the fuzzy caterpillars that the fiber is named for (chenille means "caterpillar" in French). While chenille used to be made by weaving cloth with extra strands and then cutting the cloth into pieces, today's chenille is made by spinning lengths of fiber between two main strands. The strands can be made of cotton, acrylic, silk, rayon, or other fibers.

When knit up, chenille has an incredibly plush feel, and that softness explains why it's often used for baby items and close-to-the-skin accessories. Many chenilles are made with cotton tufts, which makes the yarn machine washable. Because of the yarn's texture, it can be tougher than usual to get an even gauge, and the thickness of chenille yarn makes it more difficult to do complicated stitchwork. Chenille also tends to slip out of the knitted structure, looping back on itself so that strands of yarn poke up in odd places. Worming, as this tendency is called, is due to the structure of the yarn and its slipperiness. Chenille also may exhibit bias depending on how it's manufactured, in which case using stitch patterns with a roughly even distribution of knits and purls may help minimize the bias.

## BINDERS AND OTHER CREATIVE COMBINATIONS

One way that yarn producers create interesting new yarns is by combining two very different-looking strands and twisting them together. For example, one popular combination starts with a thick, softly spun yarn

and wraps it with a very thin thread called a *binder* (c). The binder is often made of a strong synthetic, like nylon or polyester, and helps to hold the thicker strand together, while adding interesting visual effects. Yarn companies may combine two strands regardless of relative size, not so much to hold the fiber of one strand into place but rather for artistic effect.

There really are no rules when it comes to combining plies like this. I am currently knitting with a yarn consisting of two plies: a softly spun and slightly felted colored strand, loosely wrapped with a sheer white ribbon ply. The white ply gives the colored ply a muted allover effect. I've seen yarns made with a thin metallic thread wrapped around a thicker colored yarn; yarns with a haloed yarn wrapped around multicolored strands; and strands with strings of beads or sequins loosely twisted around solid-colored yarns. The sky is truly the limit.

Since there are so many variations with these kinds of yarns, keep the basics in mind: the yarn will need to be manipulated carefully, and you'll want to be mindful you don't snag your needle tips in a thicker yarn or catch only one of the two plies. Given the unusual structure, these yarns are often best for items that will not get hard wear. Finally, stick to plainer patterns and let the yarn do the work.

## MULTITEXTURED YARN

Every couple of years, people start talking about the "magic ball," as the technique was called when I first heard of it. Knitters would take small balls of yarn left over from other projects and fasten them together, winding them

d

into one very big ball of yarn that was made up of many different kinds of yarns. As they continued to knit, the colors and texture changed like magic. Yarn manufacturers have experimented with commercial yarns that achieve a similar effect to the magic ball (d). For example, Prism Yarn makes an amazing yarn called Layers Stuff™: lengths of different types of yarn are spun together, so that the knitter works through one style of yarn for a few feet or yards, then transitions to the next style of yarn, and so on. Layers Stuff includes sections of plied yarns, ribbon, chainette, and bouclé, and a mix of fibers including nylon, cotton, cashmere, wool, nylon, and mohair.

Once again, there is so much going on with a yarn like this that fancy stitch patterns simply aren't necessary (and may be tough to execute given the frequent changes in the yarn's fiber and structure). And figuring out a static gauge may prove to be a nightmare! Let the yarn do the work and stick to less elaborate styles and stitch patterns (or patterns specifically designed for that particular yarn).

## RAILROAD TRACK YARNS

e

Line up two very thin threads of a strong synthetic, like nylon, parallel to each other. Now attach squares or flags of bright or shiny contrast colors that connect the two outside threads. Congratulations! You've got yourself a railroad track yarn (e), named for the resemblance, obviously, to the shape of train tracks (they're also called ladder yarns because the flags look like the rungs of a ladder). The center flags of yarn reflect light and add loads of color. Railroad track yarns are great for creating glitzy items like shawls and wraps for fancy occasions; for using as an accent yarn; or for stranding along with a second yarn to add color and shine.

Railroad track yarns go through bursts of popularity, but they can usually be found at a good-size yarn shop—the Plymouth Yarn Eros® line of railroad track yarns is a perennial favorite. Railroad track yarns can be tricky to knit with because the needle tip tends to get trapped in the spaces between the flags, and sometimes the thin threads don't get pulled all the way through the loops of your knitting. As with so many novelty yarns, you'll have trouble ripping out and seeing your stitches. Depending on needle size, the thin threads and spaces between the flags may make your knitted fabric see-through. It's best to keep to simple stitch patterns and basic shapes unless you've got a lot of experience knitting with these yarns.

## FLAGS, BEADS, AND OTHER DOODADS

If you like bling, you'll have a great time exploring the world of novelty yarns. One common construction is to attach decorative elements to the strand: small flags of yarn, sequins, beads, even little flowers. Some of these yarns are carry-along yarns—they consist of a very thin thread, allowing the knitter to knit a strand of the novelty yarn along with a second yarn. Carry-along yarns don't alter gauge but give extra color, shine, or festivity to a project without the knitter having to sew on beads or string sequins. Other yarns have a more traditional base and are intended for use on their own, with the beads or other attachments forming an integrated part of the yarn.

Here are some things to keep in mind when considering novelty yarns:

- Inexperienced knitters may find them challenging to work with.

- Blunt-tipped needles may help avoid splitting stitches and missing plies.

- The stickier surface of bamboo or wood needles may slow down the movement of the stitches and make the knitting easier.

- Novelty yarns, by definition, have a lot going on visually and are likely to overwhelm anything but the simplest of patterns.

- Novelty yarns can be difficult to manipulate, and thus aren't the best choice for patterns requiring multistitch decreases, cables, and the like.

- Some novelty yarns can be heavy and, if made entirely of synthetic yarns, aren't breathable.

From a substitution standpoint, the biggest challenge is the fact that novelty yarns are so unique. A garment knit in one yarn may look entirely different when knit with a different type of novelty yarn.

When substituting for a novelty yarn, analyze the design carefully. Novelty yarns are often used with simple silhouettes and basic stitch patterns so that the individuality of the yarn shines. If you substitute a plain yarn for a novelty yarn, you may find yourself with a garment that lacks the panache of the original. Likewise, if you select a novelty yarn for a pattern that is knit in a complex stitch pattern, you may find that the structural differences of a novelty yarn make it difficult to execute, while the visual complexity of the yarn overwhelms your stitchwork.

**4**

# VISUAL EFFECTS: SOLIDS, MULTIS, AND BEYOND

Color is such an integral part of a knitting design that it is a top consideration when substituting yarns. Before we wrap up our discussion on yarn, we need to consider the many colorful effects that can be dyed or spun into a yarn, and how they can affect yarn substitution.

## SOLID-COLORED YARNS

Solid-colored yarns are versatile and reliable. When you think of a solid-colored yarn, you probably think of a yarn like the one in the photo below.

This yarn has even color throughout, with no gradations in hue or tone. Solid yarns like this are made when the manufacturer purchases fiber that is all the same color and then dyes it. Sometimes manufacturers end up with a blend of fibers from sheep of different colors. In that case, the manufacturer will first bleach the undyed yarn to a uniform whiteness, and then dye it. This ensures that the end product has a true, even color, with no variations in lightness or tone.

Some fiber, such as yak and bison, only come in relatively dark colors, like charcoal or brown. In that case, the yarn company may sell the fibers in their natural colors, creating a limited palette of neutrals like beige, tan, and gray. If the yarn company wishes to offer a wider selection of colors, they may bleach the fiber and dye it. Not every type of fiber takes well to bleaching, however, and in that case, the yarn company will dye right over the unbleached natural color. You may notice when purchasing certain fibers made from exotics that the color range is more muted and complex because of the naturally dark color of the fiber.

Sometimes the processor will deliberately leave the fiber a mixture of colors, even though it could be bleached, and dye it. The result is a heathered yarn. The dye will look a little lighter in places where the underlying fiber was lighter, and darker in places where the fiber was darker. Although heathered yarns have this variation in tone, generally the effect is subtle enough for the yarn to read like a true solid when knitted up. You'll see a similar mottled effect when yarns are made of a blend of different fiber types, say, alpaca and silk. In that case, the silk fibers may be very white while the alpaca is a darker beige. This will also give a heathered effect when dyed in solid colors. Even if all the yarns in a blend are bleached, individual types of fiber may react to the dye differently, creating tonal variations like those seen in heathered yarns.

Hand-dyed yarns, which are made in small batches by individual artisans, also can be dyed in solid colors, or, perhaps I should say, *single* colors. While some dyers create solid shades that are as consistent and even as machine-dyed solids, more often their hand-painted solids show variations in color. A rich, red hand-paint may be primarily the color of a candy apple, but with places where the red gets a bit bluer (skewing toward purple) or yellower (skewing toward orange). Or the candy-apple shade may be lighter in tone in some places, darker in others. Some dyers may add very small hints of other colors in their solids. Some may leave hints of

An undyed heathered yarn has subtle gradations of color.

white. All of these hand-painted yarns will end up reading as solids, just the way heathered yarns do.

Solids are incredibly versatile. Their relatively consistent color lets the eye focus on the individual stitches. You can use a solid yarn for just about any kind of pattern—lace, cables, textural patterns, or twisted stitches. Simpler patterns like stockinette and garter also work well in solids, showcasing the classic beauty of these stitches.

Remember that it's easier to see the individual stitches and the overall pattern in light-colored solids. If you're a new knitter or working a complicated pattern, dark solids like black and navy blue will make it harder for you to see the stitches as you work them. Without being able to read the stitches, you might make more mistakes. Dark solid colors may also make it harder for others to appreciate your beautiful stitchwork. (Is it any wonder that so many cabled Aran sweaters are knit in cream-colored yarn?)

## MULTICOLORED YARNS

Substituting can get trickier when multicolored yarns are involved. Multicolored yarns come in a staggering variety of color combinations and styles. Some are created by machine and feature regular and predictable segments of different colors dyed into the yarn. Others are dyed by hand, with color segments of different lengths and/or with a more random repeat of segments. It can be very difficult to envision what a skein of multicolored yarn will look like when knit, particularly when using hand-dyed yarns. Even two balls of the same dye lot and colorway of a hand-dyed yarn may look significantly different when knit, compounding the problem.

Knitting with multicolored yarns is a subject unto itself (see my earlier book, *Sock Yarn Studio*), but when substituting yarns, remember the following general guidelines:

1.  **LOOK AT THE YARN USED IN THE SAMPLE.** Determine whether it was machine-dyed or hand-dyed. If you can examine the skein itself, determine whether it is dyed in a regular pattern of color sequences or with more random application of colors (like speckles). Think about the colors in the yarn: are they bold and bright or more muted? Keep those qualities in mind when you're looking at substitutes.

2. **MULTICOLORED YARNS ARE UNPREDICTABLE IN THE SKEIN.** Multicolored yarns, whether hand- or machine-dyed, rarely look the same in the skein or hank as they do in the finished garment. If you're lucky, the yarn shop or website will have a swatch of the yarn for you to peruse, and if you're really lucky, a complete garment to show you how the yarn looks writ large. Unless this is a very spontaneous purchase, take a little time to do some Internet research, too. Searching for the yarn and colorway name or number in a search engine or on Ravelry.com may produce photographs from other knitters who've used the yarn. You can get a rough sense of what the yarn does when knit in different stitches and gauges, perhaps giving you a clearer idea whether the yarn is right for your project.

3. **MULTICOLORED YARNS ARE UNPREDICTABLE ON THE NEEDLES.** Many multicolored yarns that are dyed in segments develop blobs or patches of colors that mass together (often called pooling). Some people love pooling and others hate it. For the rest, I suppose it depends on what the pooling looks like. When working with a multicolored yarn, particularly a hand-painted one, expect at least some pooling, and learn some effective ways to address it.

4. **USE MULTICOLORED YARNS STRATEGICALLY.** A general rule in knitting is either the yarn does the work or the knitter does the work. This is especially true with multicolored yarns. Bright multicolored yarns can drown out the intricacies of your stitch pattern as your eye flits about from one color to the next like a deranged moth. Conversely, simple stitch patterns give a wild multicolored yarn a chance to be the center of attention. There are specific techniques and types of patterns that tend to work well with multicolored yarns, such as certain kinds of slip stitches or chevron patterns. Match multicolored yarns with these kinds of patterns and swatch, swatch, swatch!

## OTHER COLOR EFFECTS

Through the miracle of modern textile manufacturing, other types of color effects exist that can affect the overall look of your project.

## MULTICOLORED PLIES

We saw earlier that many yarns are constructed of several plies twisted around each other. Yarn manufacturers can use these multiple strands to create interesting color effects. A yarn may be made up of two different-colored plies (sometimes called a marled, barberpole, or ragg yarn). The plies may be dyed different but related shades (say, light and medium gray) or can be sharply contrasting (violet and yellow). The effect can be bold or subtle, depending on whether the colors of the ply are close together or sharply contrast.

A manufacturer may combine solid and multicolored plies. The solid plies may help tone down the multicolored ones, creating a more cohesive effect; or, the solid plies may be chosen for contrast, to create a vivid effect. Or the manufacturer may up the ante and combine plies that are all multicolored. (Schoppel Wolle Zauberball® is one of my favorites, with both bold colorways and quieter ones that are a visual delight.) Remember that yarns made of two or more multicolored plies tend to have so much contrast between plies and so many color changes along each ply that they often create a busy or dramatic effect that could drown out a complex stitch pattern. As with other multicolored yarns, you'll have to judge how muted or wild the color combinations are in your specific yarn, then select a stitch pattern that will complement—or at least not fight with—the multitude of colors in your yarn.

## STRIPES AND OTHER DYED-IN-THE-WOOL PATTERNS

Self-striping yarns add color to a project without the knitter having to change yarns. They are dyed with long segments, one after the other, that stripe when knit up. When substituting for a self-striping yarn, consider the overall look of the stripes: are they a muted range of colors (perhaps a variety of neutrals from beige to gray to brown to charcoal to cream)? If so, more intricate stitch patterns may hold their own against the changing colors. If the striping consists of a sequence of rich, bright colors, the

The yarns above are made of multicolored plies, creating very different effects.

eye will be drawn to that, instead of the pattern. Also consider whether the width of the stripes is a factor contributing to the overall look of the design, and whether wider or thinner stripes, or a mixture of wide and thin stripes, would change the aesthetics of the finished garment.

You'll also want to consider how much the design relies on the yarn's striping look for its effectiveness. For example, if a design is knit with multidirectional pieces in a self-striping yarn, and you substitute a solid yarn, the design may look too plain without the visual interest created by stripes going in different directions. In that case, you'll want to look for a substitute yarn that also makes stripes. It's also worth doing some research—looking at finished garments on Ravelry.com, for example, or checking out the manufacturer's website for photos of the repeat—to make sure you know exactly what the full repeat of the striping yarn looks like. (Remember that with colorways with a long repeat, an individual skeins of yarn might not contain every single color in the color repeat, or a color may be hidden inside the skein, surprising you when you come to it.)

In addition to stripes, yarns can be dyed in special patterns that create more elaborate effects, like checkerboards, jacquard, or Fair Isle patterns, often intermingled with regular stripes. It can be a little trickier to substitute for yarns with more unique dyed-in effects and, again, you'll want to consider how much the design relies on the yarn's patterning before switching to a non-patterning yarn.

If you're tempted to use a self-striping yarn as a substitute for a solid yarn, consider whether the yarn will complement or overwhelm the pattern. Will the addition of stripes detract from a pattern or make a specific stitch pattern harder to see? Will unique construction details be lost when the eye is drawn to color changes? Maybe the pattern has strong vertical elements that will create interesting contrast with the yarn's horizontal stripes, or maybe the stripes will complement a horizontal chevron or lace pattern.

Yarns with more complex patterns like jacquard will require a bit more consideration. Stronger patterning in the stitchwork may be bold enough to hold its own when knit in a striping yarn—but add a dyed-in Fair Isle effect and the pattern gets lost. Remember, too, that patterning yarns are a bit trickier to work with. Changes in width or circumference may throw the pattern off or make it less crisp. You'll have to be flexible and play with self-patterning yarns to get an effect you like.

Note how the swatch on the right has clear, straight lines where the color changes, while the swatch on the left gradually changes color.

## GRADIENT & OMBRÉ YARNS

Gradient yarns and ombré yarns slowly morph from one color to the next. They may start with a light shade, say, pale blue, and gradually get deeper, the pale blue turning a little bit darker, then a little more, so by the end of the skein, you are knitting with deep navy. Gradients start out one color (sage green) and very slowly start to morph into a different color (sage turns a darker shade, then turns a bit grayer, and grayer still, until it ends as charcoal). Or they may cycle through several colors, changing almost imperceptibly row by row, from orange to rust to crimson to purple. True self-striping yarns have hard lines when the color changes—one row is color A and the next row suddenly shifts to color B—but gradient yarns are known for their slow color changes over many rows or rounds. You may find that the subtler color changes of a gradient give you a bit more flexibility in selecting a stitch pattern because there are no shifts of color or sharp dividing lines between stripes. Again, experiment with these yarns to get the most pleasing effect.

This gradient yarn changes color slowly over multiple rows.

Color is one aspect of yarn substitution that is very dependent on personal preference. It also can be hard to predict without getting the yarn onto the needles and knitting a good-size swatch or even starting the garment. When working with a colorful yarn, keep the following factors in mind:

- The amount and complexity of the stitchwork pattern, and how different color effects will highlight or obscure the pattern.

- The simplicity or complexity of the garment's shape and design details and how different color effects will add or detract.

- Whether a pattern relies on a specific color effect to achieve its overall look or could be knit in a solid-colored yarn without looking drab.

Now take one last look at your lists, considering the effect of different types of color effects in the yarn you used. Was a solid color the perfect choice for an intricate textural pattern? Did a marled yarn cause the cables in a sweater to get lost in the shuffle? Did the pooling of a hand-painted yarn leave you dissatisfied with your socks? Did switching to a self-striping yarn add pizzazz to a cowl or shawl? Make notes about your choices and keep them in mind when considering yarns with various color effects.

**5**

# CLASSIFICATION: PUTTING YARN IN ITS PLACE

While you may be eager to get right to the substituting, there's one more important topic we need to cover: how yarns are classified in the knitting world. When I rediscovered knitting as an adult, I didn't understand how yarns were sorted into different categories—or why it mattered so much. That made it difficult to pick the right yarn for the projects I wanted to make—and I have the half-finished pieces to prove it!

> I learned the hard way that understanding the yarn classification system is essential if you want to substitute yarns successfully.

Side benefit: You'll feel more confident and in control when you're yarn shopping, and you'll have a clearer idea what to do with yarn you purchased without a specific pattern in mind.

As we work our way through this section of the book, we're going to build ourselves a handy-dandy chart with all the information you need to know about yarn classification. The chart is loosely based on the yarn classification system created by the Craft Yarn Council (CYC), an industry association.

The CYC's Standard Yarn Weight System is shown online at craft-yarncouncil.com/standards/yarn-weight-system. Through the years, I've come to appreciate how logical this yarn classification system is and how helpful it is to have clearly delineated categories that the entire industry can use. For consistency's sake, our chart adopts the eight categories established by the CYC, beginning with category 0 and going all the way through category 7.

## WHY 0 TO 7?

When the CYC system first was created, it contained only six categories of yarn: categories 1 through 6. The original category 1 combined fingering-weight yarns and lace-weight yarns. Because these types of yarn behave differently on the needles—lace-weight yarns are considerably thinner and lighter than fingering-weight yarns—the chart was revised to give each its own category. A new category 0 was added for the finest group of yarns, such as lace and cobweb yarns, while fingering-weight yarns remained in category 1.

For many years, category 6 contained the thickest group of yarns. When the arm-knitting craze began a few years ago, manufacturers began creating super-thick yarns—far thicker than could be comfortably knit using regular-size needles. The CYC responded by creating category 7 for these jumbo-size yarns. And that is why this eight-category system begins with category 0 and ends with category 7, instead of going from 1 to 8 as you might expect.

| CATEGORY 0 | CATEGORY 1 | CATEGORY 2 | CATEGORY 3 | CATEGORY 4 | CATEGORY 5 | CATEGORY 6 | CATEGORY 7 |
|---|---|---|---|---|---|---|---|
| Lace | Superfine | Fine | Light | Medium | Bulky | Super Bulky | Jumbo |
| Lace-weight, cobweb, crochet thread, 2-ply | Fingering, sock, 4-ply, baby | Sport, baby | DK (double-knitting), light worsted | Worsted, light vs. heavy worsted, Aran | Chunky, bulky | Superchunky, polar | Arm knitting yarn |
| 8 or more sts per inch but variable | 7–8 sts per inch | 6–7 sts per inch | 5–6 sts per inch | 4–5 sts per inch | 3–4 sts per inch | 2–3 sts per inch | Fewer than 2 sts per inch |
| US or smaller (variable— US 4–9) | US 0–3 | US 3–5 | US 5–7 | US 7–9 | US 9–13 | US 13–17 | Larger than US 17 |
| More than 210 yds/50g | 180–210 yds/50g | 150–180 yds/50g | 120–150 yds/50g | 90–120 yds/50g | 60–90 yds/50g | 30–60 yds/50g | Fewer than 30 yds/50g |

At the top row of our chart, you'll see the category numbers established by the CYC, along with the CYC's skein-shaped symbols. (These symbols, with the category number on the skein's "label," are intended for use in printed patterns and on yarn labels to make a yarn's category easily identifiable.) The second row on our chart sets out the category names used by the CYC. For example, category 0 is Lace, category 1 is Superfine, and on through category 7, Jumbo.

While the CYC has assigned names for each category, many knitters know these categories by different names. I am accustomed to calling category 4 yarns "worsted-weight" yarns, for instance, instead of "medium." To help you keep the names straight, the third row of our chart lists the most common names for each category of yarn.

## PLY AND YARN WEIGHT

In the last chapter, we discussed plied yarns and, specifically, how some yarns are made by combining multiple plies (page 54). Many years ago, when textile manufacturing was less technologically developed, mills would spin a single standard strand of yarn. They would then "build" their yarns by combining different numbers of these standard strands, or plies, together. A yarn made of two plies was approximately lace weight (0); a yarn made of four plies was fingering weight (1); a yarn made of six plies was sport weight (2), and so on. Every time the mill added two strands to the yarn, it became thicker by one category.

| | |
|---|---|
| Category 0: Lace | 2 plies (cobweb yarn consists of 1 strand) |
| Category 1: Superfine | 4 plies |
| Category 2: Fine | 6 plies |
| Category 3: Light | 8 plies |
| Category 4: Medium | 10 plies |
| Category 5: Bulky | 12 plies |
| Category 6: Super Bulky | 14 plies |
| Category 7: Jumbo | N/A |

In the past, many yarn makers incorporated the number of plies they used in the yarn's name. Because the size of the ply remained consistent, the number of plies could be used as shorthand for the yarn's category.

Today you may still see yarn names that include the number of plies, such as Rowan Summerlite 4-ply or Jamieson & Smith 2-ply Jumper Weight. These yarns use "4-ply" or "2-ply" to describe the category of the yarn—fingering weight and lace weight, respectively—as opposed to the number of plies in the yarn construction. (You more frequently will see these ply designations in yarn names when the manufacturer is based in the United Kingdom, Australia, or New Zealand.) When you see a ply designation on a yarn label, look carefully to determine whether it is referring to the yarn's category, whether it actually is describing the yarn's construction, or both.

## THICKNESS

Now that we've got our chart set up, let's talk about how we put specific yarns into each category. The most obvious way to sort yarns is by their relative thickness. Yarns can be as thin as dental floss or as thick as a garden hose. Because it makes sense to categorize yarns according to thickness, the categories on our chart are arranged that way, with the thinnest yarns in category 0, at the far left, and the thickest ones in category 7, at the far right.

While thickness is a logical way to categorize yarns, there's one big problem: it's not precise. I can look at one yarn and say, "This is thick," and at another and say, "This yarn is thinner than the first," but exactly *how much* thinner is it? I know that category 3 yarns are thicker than category 2 yarns, but how much thicker? I can look at a particular yarn and know that because it's relatively thin, I need a small needle size, but should I use a US size 1 or a size 3 or a size 4?

Precision is critical when it comes to knitting. We want to be able to predict and control the size of our knitted projects. If we're making clothing—garments meant to fit specific people—we need precision to ensure that the garments fit their intended wearer. While we can eyeball a yarn's thickness to some extent, a visual estimate isn't accurate enough to help us create well-fitting knitwear.

Yarns can be sorted by thickness, but this method isn't precise.

## WRAPS PER INCH

One method designed to measure a yarn's thickness uses units called "wraps per inch," or WPI. To measure wraps per inch, you need a rigid measuring device like a wooden ruler. (Gadget manufacturers make special tools for measuring wraps per inch, too.) You take a strand of the yarn you'd like to identify and gently wrap it around the ruler between the two marks that measure out one inch. The goal is to wrap the strand as many times as you can between the marks without stretching the yarn tightly or letting it flop loosely. Each strand must sit next to its neighbor, just barely touching but not crammed in too close, without a large amount of space in between. You then count the number of strands (or wraps) per inch and compare the number to a standard chart to determine the yarn's category.

I've never particularly liked the WPI system for several reasons. The first two relate to the accuracy of the measurement. How tightly you wrap the stitches around the ruler can affect the accuracy of the measurement. If you pull hard and stretch the yarn, each strand will be thinner, possibly causing more wraps to fit into the inch. Second, an accurate WPI measurement assumes that you will space the wraps just right—not too close together and not too far apart. If your spacing differs from the norm, you will get an inaccurate measurement with more or fewer wraps than you should have. The nail in the coffin for me: I've found no clear consensus among the various charts that purport to set out the equivalencies between wraps per inch and category. If you are getting, say, 12 wraps per inch, three different equivalency charts may give you three different categories that correspond to 12 wraps per inch. Not helpful!

I know that many hand-spinners view WPI as a tool to help them identify the category of their hand-spun yarn, and wraps per inch may be accurate enough to provide a ballpark estimate of a yarn's category. I prefer not to rely on WPI measurements for purposes of yarn substitution, however, because I don't feel confident that they are precise enough.

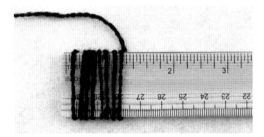

Luckily, we have a technique that enables us to quantify the thickness or thinness of each particular yarn and to make meaningful comparisons among different yarns. That technique is measuring gauge.

## GAUGE

All hail gauge, the magical technique that gives us a precise way to measure our knitting and classify yarns! Whether we pick or throw, whether we hold the working yarn in the right or left hand, whether we're tight knitters or loose knitters or medium knitters, gauge is there for us. It allows us to compare the size of our knitting with the size called for by the pattern and to adjust our knitting as necessary so that our finished projects are the sizes we want them to be.

Despite its importance, there's a lot of fake news out there about gauge. To make sure we're all on the same page, let's review some frequently asked questions about gauge measurements.

### 1. WHAT IS GAUGE?

Gauge is a way to measure the size of your stitches. The concept is simple: You knit a swatch using the project yarn and needles in an appropriate size. Next you measure the size of your stitches and the size of your rows (or rounds, if you're knitting circularly). Compare those measurements with the measurements used in the pattern. If they match, you're good to go. If your stitches are bigger or smaller, you reknit the swatch, adjusting the needle size until they do match.

### 2. DO I *HAVE TO* MAKE A GAUGE SWATCH?

In a word, yes, you really do have to knit a gauge swatch. Making a gauge swatch can seem like a lot of fuss, but rest assured it is indeed essential to create garments that fit. Consider a basic cap. Suppose the pattern tells you to cast on 100 stitches to make your hat, and requires that you knit at a gauge of 5 stitches per inch. If you are in fact knitting at the proper gauge, you'll end up with a hat that is approximately 20 inches in circumference—the perfect size for most adults (100 stitches divided by 5 stitches per inch = 20 inches). But imagine you are knitting at a gauge of 4 stitches per inch, just one stitch per inch less than the requested gauge. Your cap would measure 25 inches around—perfect for a pumpkin, but way too large for most people. If your actual gauge was 6 stitches per inch, just one stitch per inch more than the requested gauge, your hat would measure about 16½ inches in circumference—a great fit for a small child but way too small for an adult. One stitch off in either direction turns a perfect fit into a knitting nightmare.

Gauge swatches help you not only get an accurate accurte fit, but also show how a substitute yarn will look when knit in the appropriate stitch pattern.

### 3. HOW BIG SHOULD MY GAUGE SWATCH BE?

Opinions diverge on the precise measurements needed for an accurate gauge swatch. I have heard industry professionals advise knitting a gauge swatch as small as 4 inches square and as large as one foot square—quite a difference! Since the whole point of knitting a swatch is to get an accurate gauge measurement, you'll need to knit a good-sized swatch to ensure that you have enough knitting to measure. Typically that means a swatch with a *minimum* size of 6 inches by 6 inches. You may need to knit an even wider swatch if your stitch pattern has extra-long repeats because you'll need to include the entire length of the stitch pattern to get an accurate gauge measurement. Look at your swatching as "risk management." (Sorry, I'm a lawyer in my day job.) The more care you take in measuring gauge, the more you'll reduce the risk of a finished garment that doesn't fit.

### 4. HOW DO I KNOW WHAT NEEDLE SIZE TO USE FOR MY GAUGE SWATCH?

Use the needle size that is recommended for your yarn (usually listed on the label or the manufacturer's website) or the needle size used in the pattern—they should be the same or very close. If your swatch's gauge doesn't match the pattern gauge and you need to adjust, there is a general rule of thumb: to change one whole stitch per inch, most knitters need to go up or down two needle sizes. (To put it another way, switching from one needle size to the next usually changes gauge by ½ stitch per inch.)

Suppose your pattern calls for a gauge of 6 stitches and 8 rows per inch. You knit a gauge swatch on a size 7 needle and your gauge measures 5 stitches and 7 rows per inch. The pattern requires you to get more stitches per inch (6) than you're getting (5). That means you need smaller stitches, and therefore you'll need to switch to a smaller needle size. You need to change your gauge by one whole stitch per inch (from 5 to 6 stitches per inch), so I'd advise trying a size 5 needle next. *Remember that this is a general guideline only*—you must swatch to make sure the new needle size gets the gauge you need. Knowing this general rule, however, may help minimize the number of needles that you need to try before getting your desired gauge.

## 5. SHOULD I KNIT A BORDER AROUND MY SWATCH?

I've said before that knitters can debate just about everything, and I've heard heated discussions concerning borders on gauge swatches. The pro-border contingent asserts that a border ensures a more accurate gauge measurement by firmly anchoring all the edge stitches in the swatch. Each knitted stitch looks like the letter V, with left and right "arms." Stitches located in the middle of the swatch have arms that are intertwined with the neighboring stitches on both sides. That keeps the stitch in place and makes it unlikely to stretch out. Edge stitches, however, have only one arm anchored to a neighboring stitch. The other arm has no anchor; it's just hanging there in space. The idea is that those edge stitches, only half anchored, are looser and can stretch out the stitches nearby, distorting the gauge measurement. If the swatch has a border, the knitter can measure only the pattern stitch (the "picture" inside the "frame" of the border), and all of these inside stitches will be anchored on both sides by a neighboring stitch.

The potential problem with borders, however, is that you are introducing a new stitch pattern, with its own gauge, into your swatch. You must be very careful to ensure that the row gauge of the border stitch isn't different from the row gauge of the pattern stitch. If the row gauge of the border stitch is more compact or more elongated than the row gauge of the pattern stitch, it can condense or expand the stitches, giving a misleading measurement. This is why garter stitch is not the best border to use when measuring gauge. Garter stitch has a very dense row gauge compared to most other stitches. A garter-stitch border may pull the pattern stitches together, giving an incorrect gauge measurement. (You can see this in the swatch below.) In contrast, seed or moss stitch has a less dense row gauge and is much less likely to affect row gauge (below).

Note how the garter stitch edges of the swatch are condensed, pulling the rows of stockinette stiches into each other and distorting row gauge.

In the swatches used for this book, I alternated between garter stitch and moss stitch edgings. Garter stitch is faster and easier, and these swatches are not going to be used to fit a specific garment, so I took some liberties.

## 6. WHAT STITCH PATTERN SHOULD I USE TO KNIT THE SWATCH? WHAT IF THE PATTERN CALLS FOR MORE THAN ONE STITCH PATTERN IN THE GAUGE MEASUREMENT?

A well-written pattern will describe in the gauge section what pattern stitch is being used to measure gauge. You should use that one in your swatch:

**GAUGE**
19 sts/28 rows = 4"/10cm over St st

In the vast majority of cases, you'll need to swatch in the particular stitch pattern used for the garment. Many patterns call for a different stitch for edgings than for the body of the garment, like an inch of ribbing at hem and cuffs. Patterns do not generally include a specific gauge measurement for such small amounts of an additional stitch pattern as ribbed edgings. Occasionally a design will use two different pattern stitches, each of which is used for a large portion of the knitted fabric, and the pattern will include separate gauge measurements for each pattern. In this case, make sure to swatch both stitch patterns, changing needle size if required.

Here is a typical swatch knit in stockinette stitch.

Start by taking the horizontal measurement: the number of stitches that fit into an inch, called stitch gauge. Place the swatch on a flat surface, then place the measuring device on the swatch. Find the markings that show the beginning and end of an inch. Now imagine the inch markings going all the way up in a straight line. Carefully count the exact number of stitches in the row that fit within your imaginary lines. For example, in this swatch, you can count 5 stitches falling within the inch markings. The stitch gauge of this swatch is 5 stitches per inch.

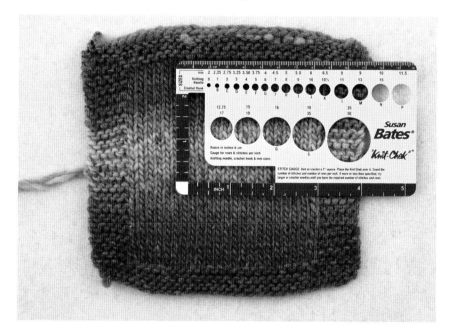

Use a measuring tool like this one to determine stitch and row gauge.

Using a swatch gauge next you'll take the vertical measurement: the number of rows (or rounds) that fit into an inch, commonly called row gauge. Place the measuring device on your swatch vertically and find the markings that show the beginning and end of an inch. Again, imagine the inch markings going all the way across in straight lines. Carefully count the exact number of rows or rounds that fit within your imaginary lines. For example, in this swatch, you can count 7 rows falling within the inch markings. The row gauge of this swatch is 7 rows per inch.

Now compare the gauge you are getting—5 stitches and 7 rows per inch, or 20 stitches and 28 rows over 4 inches—with the gauge that the pattern calls for. If the stars align perfectly and the angels are beaming down upon you, they will be the same and you can begin the project, using the needles you used for the swatch. If not, figure out the difference (in stitches and rows) between your gauge and the pattern gauge, and reknit the swatch with bigger or smaller needles. Lather, rinse, repeat until you match gauge.

## 8. WHERE SHOULD I MEASURE THE STITCHES TO GET MY GAUGE MEASUREMENT?

Most professionals advise measuring somewhere in the center of the swatch. By keeping away from the edges, you eliminate the risk that either the border stitch pattern (if you opt for a border around your swatch) or the looser end stitches (if you do not use a border) will distort your measurement.

Another technique, helpful if you knit a very generous-size swatch, is to take several measurements at different places in the swatch and see if they all match. If they do, you'll know you're getting a consistent gauge throughout your knitting. If you're using a yarn that is unevenly spun, such as a thick-and-thin yarn, this technique can help you achieve a more accurate gauge measurement that takes into account the varying width of the yarn. Take multiple gauge measurements at different places throughout the swatch and average them. Places where the yarn is very thin will be averaged out by places where the yarn is very thick.

## 9. WHAT IF MY STITCH GAUGE IS CORRECT, BUT I CAN'T GET THE ROW GAUGE TO MATCH THE PATTERN?

Ideally, we would like to match *both* stitch and row gauge, and most knitters manage to do this most of the time. If you're getting stitch gauge but your row gauge doesn't match, try switching to needles that are the same size but made of a different material (for example, you might switch from wooden needles to metal ones). Sometimes switching needles like this helps just enough to enable you to get row gauge without altering the stitch gauge.

If that doesn't work, focus on matching the stitch gauge. The reason: if you can match stitch gauge, you usually can fudge the row gauge. Remember that knitting begins with a set of cast-on stitches. The cast-on stitches are the horizontal anchor for the piece. Once we start knitting, the horizontal measurement of the piece is set. But the vertical measurement of the piece is not fixed. We are working upward, and so we can stop whenever we like, adding or unraveling rows as needed until we have the right-sized piece. Use the schematic to figure out how many inches you need to knit, and then stop when you get to that measurement.

## ADJUSTING THE KNITTING FOR A DIFFERENT ROW GAUGE

If you have to adjust your knitting to compensate for a different row gauge, keep two things in mind. First, if your row gauge is denser (i.e., you are knitting more rows than called for by the pattern gauge), you'll have to knit more rows to get to the correct vertical measurement. More rows means more knitting means more yarn. Remember to pick up additional yarn to compensate for the fact that you are going to be working more rows than the designer did for the sample garment.

Second, if your pattern has any vertical design elements, you may have to do some calculating to make sure that the overall effect is unchanged. For example, if you are knitting a sweater that requires you to work waist shaping halfway up the body, you'll have to make sure you work the waist shaping by using inches rather than rows, so that the waist shaping isn't too high or too low because of your different row gauge. You may have to adjust vertical patterns like cables, too, so that you don't lop off an element in the middle of the pattern repeat, giving an unfinished effect.

## 10. SHOULD I BLOCK MY SWATCH?

To get an accurate measurement, you must treat your swatch exactly the way you would treat the garment you are making when it comes to washing and blocking. If you are knitting a sweater in pieces and plan to steam block them, then steam block your swatch *before measuring*. If you are knitting a lace shawl that will require a good soaking and a vigorous blocking, you'll need to soak your swatch and block it, too, before measuring gauge. (Remember to measure the gauge before blocking, so you have a reference point for checking the gauge on your unblocked work as you go along.) Some yarns change gauge when they are washed and/or blocked, and you need to know this before you cast on, so you can make any necessary adjustments in size.

We could devote many more pages to gauge, and I hope you'll take a class on gauge or look at some of the resources on page 165. Having reviewed the basics, we're ready to see how gauge fits into our overall system of yarn classification.

## STANDARD GAUGE RANGES

Until now, we've looked at gauge primarily as a method of ensuring fit. Gauge is also very important when it comes to yarn classification. We can distinguish between one yarn and another based on how many stitches per inch each yarn knits, and we can use this information to sort yarns into categories. Each category of yarn has a typical range of gauges that work best for those yarns—a gauge proportional to the thickness of the yarn, which yields a knitted fabric that is neither too tight and dense, nor too loose and sloppy.

Let's start with worsted-weight yarn (category 4). Think about the last time you knit with worsted-weight yarn. About how many stitches to the inch did you get? I'm going to guess that most readers would say they were knitting at a gauge somewhere between 4 and 5 stitches per inch (16 to 20 stitches per 4 inches). This is, in fact, the typical gauge range for a category 4 yarn. Moving across our chart (page 79) to the right, you'll see:

- Category 5 (Bulky), knitting between 3 and 4 stitches per inch

- Category 6 (Super Bulky), knitting between 2 and 3 stitches per inch

- Category 7 (Jumbo), knitting at fewer than 2 stitches per inch

Category 7 will have a greater variety of gauges, since this category includes any yarn that is thicker than category 6, and that could theoretically include some very thick yarns indeed.

Going back to category 4 and moving to the left, you'll see:

- Category 3 (Light), knitting between 5 and 6 stitches per inch

- Category 2 (Fine), knitting between 6 and 7 stitches per inch

- Category 1 (Superfine), knitting between 7 and 8 stitches per inch

Category 0 (Lace) is a little trickier than the others. If we were knitting stockinette stitch to create a typical fabric—with stitches that are not too tight and crammed together, and stitches that are not especially loose with big holes between them—you would find that this category knit at 8 or more stitches per inch. However, the lace-weight category is a little special. We generally use category 0 yarns knit at larger-than-typical gauges, using eyelets and decreases and other spread-out patterns, then block them vigorously. If you're knitting your stitch pattern loosely so you can block it vigorously, then you might get anywhere from 4 to 7 stitches per inch, especially after aggressive blocking. For these reasons, I've included both the "8 stitches or more per inch" range and "variable," to show that category 0 yarns are often used quite differently than other categories.

Step back a bit and look at the chart. What we find is that each category on our yarn classification chart has a typical range of stitches per inch—a gauge where the yarn performs optimally, creating a fabric that is not too stiff and not too holey. Yes, there are times when we use yarns in unusual ways, deviating from the typical gauge range (and we'll talk about that in a minute), but generally, these gauge ranges are a reliable and precise way to differentiate between different categories of yarn. That makes gauge an essential part of yarn classification.

When you scan the different categories on the chart and see their typical gauges, you'll see that the smaller the yarn, the more stitches that can fit in an inch, and the thicker the yarn, the fewer stitches can fit into an inch. This makes sense. There's more fiber in thicker yarn and it's larger in diameter than thinner yarn, so it stands to reason that it would make bigger stitches. Bigger stitches take up more room, so there are fewer of them in an inch of knitting. Thinner stitches are skinnier, and you can fit more of them in the same inch of knitting.

## NEEDLE SIZE

Just as each category of yarn has a typical gauge range, it also has a range of typical needle sizes. This makes sense: as the yarns in each category get progressively thicker, they require thicker needles. Note, too, that needle size changes by about the same amount as you move from category to category.

Let's start with worsted-weight yarn again. What size needles would you use if you were knitting with a worsted-weight (category 4) yarn? The typical range of needle sizes used with a category 4 yarn is approximately US size 7 to 9.

Watch as the needle size range changes by set increments from category to category. Moving to the right, you'll see:

- Category 5 (Bulky), knitting with approximately US size 9 to 13 needles

- Category 6 (Super Bulky), knitting with approximately US size 13 to 17 needles

- Category 7 (Jumbo), knitting with needles larger than US size 17 (or arms!)

Category 7 will have a greater variety of needle sizes used, since it includes any yarn that needs a needle larger than size 17, going all the way up to yarns that require needles the size of tree trunks.

Going back to category 4 and moving to the left, you'll see

- Category 3 (Light), knitting with approximately US size 5 to 7 needles

- Category 2 (Fine), knitting with approximately US size 3 to 5 needles

- Category 1 (Superfine), knitting with approximately US size 0 to 3 needles

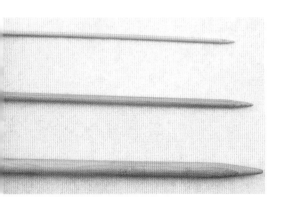

Needle circumference can vary substantially but, as general rule, the thicker the yarn, the thicker the needle required.

Once again, category 0 (Lace) is a little trickier than the others. If we were continuing the progression and knitting stockinette stitch at a comfortable gauge, we'd probably end up on a size US 000 to 0.

Because we usually knit these yarns at expanded gauges, in practice the needle size range varies from approximately US size 3 all the way on up to US size 7 or more, depending on the exact diameter of the yarn and the intended effect.

Never again will you look at a skein of yarn and ask, "What needle size should I use?" Once you know what category the yarn is, you will know right away what range of needle sizes will work with the yarn (assuming it's not being used in an atypical way).

## WEIGHT

In addition to thickness and gauge, there is a third factor that helps us categorize yarn: weight. We can use the ratio of length to weight (yards/grams per skein) to categorize yarns and compare them to each other. Imagine that we have two skeins of yarn. One contains lace-weight yarn (category 0) and the other contains bulky-weight yarn (category 5). Now imagine measuring off one yard from each skein. The strand of lace-weight yarn is much thinner than the strand of bulky-weight yarn. We can see that it contains much less fiber than the bulkier yarn. If we weigh it, we'll find that it weighs substantially less than the yard of bulky yarn. This shouldn't be a surprise: thinner yarns have less fiber in them so they weigh less, and bulky yarns contain more fiber so they weigh more.

Yarn shops tend not to sell yarn in one-yard lengths, of course, but in skeins or hanks of a certain standard weight. (How a yarn is packaged for retail, both in terms of how it's presented and how much it weighs, is called the put-up.) The put-up for most retail yarns is a skein of either 50 grams or 100 grams.

## WHAT HAPPENED TO OUNCES?

If you have been knitting awhile or use older patterns, you may be used to weighing skeins of yarn in ounces rather than grams. Many companies still do use imperial measurements (most American knitters think of their yarn in terms of yards, not meters) on their labels, but nearly all have added metric equivalents. Because most other countries have converted to the metric system, the trend of measuring yarn in meters and grams is going to continue. Use a search engine to find an ounce-to-gram converter if the yarn label doesn't include both.

If you compare skeins of equal weight across the eight categories on our chart, you'll find that there is a standard range of yardage for the yarns in each category. For example, when sock yarn is sold in a single skein, with enough to knit a pair of average-size socks, you'll find there are around 400 yards, give or take, in a 100-gram skein. Some skeins may have 385 yards, others 410 yards, but the yardage of most category 1 yarns falls into the 370 to 420 yards range for a 100-gram skein.

Let's look at our yarn classification chart. Just as each category of yarn has a standard range for gauge and a range of typical needle sizes, so each category has a standard range of yardage per unit of measurement. In our chart, we use 50 grams as our standard unit of measurement, because most yarns are sold in 50-gram balls or hanks.

Starting once again at category 4, worsted weight (or medium, as the CYC calls it), the standard number of yards per 50-gram skein is somewhere between 90 and 120. (As before, these are rough estimates, and individual yarns may vary a bit from these ranges.) Moving to the right, category 5, bulky yarns, contains somewhere between 60 and 90 yards, and category 6, superbulky, contains between 30 and 60 yards per 50-gram ball. When we get to category 7, jumbo yarn, we'll say that the range is fewer than 30 yards per 50-gram ball. As we've seen before, we'll find a bit more variation with the categories on each end of the chart, since these end categories include more yarns. While a super-bulky yarn (category 6) may have 20 or 25 yards per 50-gram skein, yarns in category 7 that are substantially larger in diameter may have only a few yards in a 50-gram skein. These yarns are often sold in cones or larger-than-typical put-ups of several hundred grams to provide enough yardage for a cowl or other small project.

Going in the other direction, category 3 tends to have somewhere between 120 and 150 yards per 50-gram skein; category 2 between 150 and 180 yards per 50-gram skein; and category 1, from 180 to 210 yards per 50-gram ball. As with category 7 yarns, lace-weight yarns are often sold in put-ups other than 50 grams to provide enough yardage for small projects without having to join in a new ball of yarn, but 50 grams of category 0 yarn could have 500 or more yards in it.

Weight to yardage tends to be a very reliable measure of a yarn's category, even absent other information like the yarn's average gauge or needle size. If you end up with a skein of mystery yarn, with no label or other identifying information, figuring out how many yards per unit of weight it contains will give you a reliable estimate of the yarn's weight.

## FIGURING OUT YARDAGE TO WEIGHT

If you've got a mystery yarn and no idea how many yards are in the skein, there are ways to find out. First weigh the yarn (postal scales work well for this). Then determine about how many yards are in the skein. If you have an umbrella swift, you can open it to a circumference of 2 yards. Wind the skein around and count the loops. Multiply by 2 and you'll have a relatively accurate estimate of yardage. Or you can use a niddy noddy (a spinning tool that looks like the capital letter *I*) and wind off the yarn to measure its yardage. *Voilá!* Compare that yards to weight ratio to our chart to find the yarn's approximate category.

Every so often you'll run into a yarn that is, for whatever reason, mislabeled. I fell in love with a yarn, long discontinued, that was labeled as a DK-weight yarn, but contained 190 yards per 50-gram skein. Skeptical, I knit it on various needle sizes and concluded that no matter what the label said, this yarn was a fingering weight that liked to knit at around 7 stitches per inch on a US size 2 needle. A ratio of 190 yards per 50-gram skein falls squarely into the fingering-weight category (category 1), and, sure enough, that's what the yarn behaved like. To this day, I still believe the yarn was mislabeled through some quirk of the process, and you will never convince me otherwise!

# II
# THE
# SUBSTITUTION
# PROCESS

**SWAPPING YARNS**

Now that you've mastered the basics about yarn and gauge, you're ready to start substituting. We'll start by considering reasons for substituting yarn, then evaluate the qualities of the original yarn used in the sample. Finally, we'll walk through an easy and logical approach to the nitty-gritty of the substitution process (including how to use simple worksheets to keep track of your options).

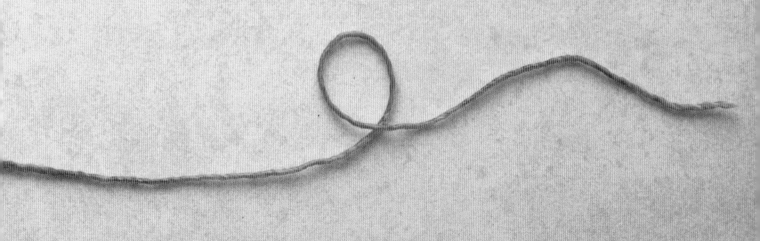

# 6 WHY SUBSTITUTE?

Let's start with a very important question: Why do you want to substitute yarns in the first place? Maybe it's a simple reason—the yarn used in the sample is discontinued. Maybe it's a combination of reasons—you prefer wool to alpaca, you aren't crazy about the colors used, and you've got a limited budget. Maybe you just want to see what your options are before you commit to a sweater's worth of yarn. You'll find some common reasons for substitution below.

- Cost
- Fiber allergy or sensitivity
- Climate
- Brand loyalty
- Lack of availability
- Using up yarn in your stash
- Personal tendency to feel cold or warm
- Machine washability
- Personal preferences
- Using a vintage pattern
- Dislike for the original yarn
- Color
- Social or political reasons

Whatever your motivation, write the specific reasons at the top of your worksheet. When it comes time for yarn shopping, reviewing your priorities will focus your mind and help narrow what may seem like an unlimited number of choices.

## STUDY THE ORIGINAL YARN

Look for the CVC symbol identifying the yarn's category.

Before you can pick a good substitute, you must know what you're replacing. Start by collecting all the information you can about the original yarn from the pattern. Look for the most important piece of information you'll need to make a good choice: the CYC category of the original yarn (left). If you're lucky, the pattern will include the little skein symbol with the number inside (or words like Category 1) and you'll know right away what category of yarn was used for the sample.

## CATEGORY

If the pattern doesn't tell you the correct category, use what you learned in Part I to determine the yarn's category. See if the pattern describes the yarn using a category name (e.g., "this fingering-weight yarn"), and check the ratio of yards to grams, referring back to our yarn category chart (page 79). If you aren't quite sure, use a search engine to find the manufacturer's website or another reliable source.

Once you determine the original yarn's category number, write it at the top of your worksheet. Circle it, highlight it, make giant red arrows pointing to it—this is the most important piece of information you'll need when yarn shopping.

What's the big deal about category number, you ask? We saw earlier how yarns come in different thicknesses, and that different-sized yarns will make different-sized stitches. If your stitches are a different size than the designer's stitches, then you're going to end up with a different-sized garment—which both defeats the whole purpose of gauge measurement and prevents a good fit.*

---

* It's true that yarn category is somewhat flexible for certain types of projects. Shawls and scarves, for example, are flat pieces and are wrapped around the wearer, eliminating fit issues. In these cases, switching yarn categories is less fraught with danger. You will have to think about the ultimate size of the finished project if you switch yarn categories (bigger yarn creates bigger finished items and smaller yarn creates smaller items). You should also remember that you may need to adjust the yarn quantity if you change categories. Finally, the aesthetic issues described in the following pages may be a factor.

Even if you do get the same gauge from yarn in a different category, your finished project will not be the same as the sample, even though the garment may fit. Designers select a category of yarn for very specific reasons, considering the heaviness of the knitted fabric, its thickness, and the overall aesthetics of yarns in this category. You may be able to force the substitute yarn to give you the pattern's correct gauge, but it's very likely that the knitted fabric you get will not look or behave like the yarn shown in the sample. Consider the three swatches below. Each was knit to a gauge of 5 stitches per inch on 30 stitches. The swatch in the center was knit using a category 4 (worsted weight) yarn. A gauge of 5 stitches per inch is the typical gauge for this category, and the yarn looks and behaves just as you would expect it to: not too tight, not too loose. Like Goldilocks's porridge, it's just right.

The swatch on the left was knit using a category 1 (fingering weight) yarn, a much thinner yarn. Although the yarn is knit at the same gauge, it looks very different than the category 4 yarn. The stitches are bigger and looser, and the holes inside the stitches are very prominent. This swatch has drape, since the stitches can slide past each other and back easily, but it is quite a bit lighter and less opaque. The swatch on the right was knit with a category 5 (bulky) yarn. Although the yarn was knit to the gauge of 5 stitches per inch, the individual stitches are crammed together. The fabric is very stiff and can almost stand up by itself. It was actually a bit difficult to knit, too, because the loops of yarn were so tight.

If you translate these results to knitted garments, you can readily see why a switch in category can cause a dramatic change in the look and feel of your finished project. A shawl that looks floaty and airy when knit in a lighter-weight yarn will look heavy and ponderous in a chunky yarn. A stitch pattern can look delicate when knit at a finer gauge but lose that effect when knit with a heavy yarn. A sweater that is knit in a heavier yarn will certainly be warmer, but you may not be able to move around too well when wearing it because the fabric is so stiff. Using the wrong category of yarn is like wearing the wrong size of shoes: you can force your feet into them, but you're going to have trouble walking comfortably.*

If you remember nothing else about the process of yarn substitution, please remember this:

**For best results, you must select a substitute yarn that is the same category as the yarn used in the original pattern.**

## WHY USE CATEGORY INSTEAD OF GAUGE?

We use the category number of the yarn, instead of needle size or gauge, because category number doesn't change—it's built into the yarn. Gauge and needle size, however, do sometimes change. Occasionally a designer will deviate from the usual gauge range for a yarn. A few years ago, I was asked to design a sweater using a sport-weight (category 2) yarn. The yarn company requested a looser-than-typical gauge so the sweater would have a light, ethereal quality and more drape than was typical for this all-wool yarn. Instead of a gauge of 6 to 7 stitches per inch on a size US 3 to 5 needle—the typical gauge and needle size for a sport-weight yarn—I used a size 7 needle to get a gauge of about 5 stitches per inch. The bigger needle created larger, looser stitches to achieve the special effect that the yarn company wanted. Suppose you looked at this pattern and didn't note the yarn's category number, but instead relied on needle size and gauge to pick the substitute's category. With a gauge of 5 stitches per inch and a size 7 needle, you would think the original yarn was a worsted-weight (category 4) yarn. If you knit this pattern in a worsted-weight yarn, you would get a very different result. You'd have a fabric that was not particularly airy or loose, but about average. That would change the delicate look of the sweater. The fabric itself would be thicker, changing the way it fit the wearer in subtle ways (and making it warmer!). Because needle size and gauge can vary, you must rely on the category number to replicate the kind of fabric and the feel of the design shown in the sample.

---

* Students often ask me if it's possible to substitute a different weight of yarn and then adapt the pattern to the new weight. This is a wholly different process than switching the yarn. Depending on the type of garment, its structure, and its complexity, this can quickly turn into a difficult project, requiring you to essentially rewrite the pattern and possibly make extensive changes to it. It's a topic all its own and beyond the scope of this book.

## FIBER CONTENT, CONSTRUCTION, AND APPEARANCE

Once you've noted the category number, study other aspects of the original yarn, thinking about how well the yarn's characteristics serve the needs of the pattern. Begin by asking questions about the fiber content: What fiber or blend of fibers did the designer select? What are the characteristics of that type of fiber? Are these characteristics integral to the design? For example, suppose the designer selected a silk/rayon blend. You now know that this type of yarn blend has excellent movement and drape. Look at the pattern itself: does it rely on the flow of a draping yarn as part of its appeal? If so, you'll want to note "drape" on your worksheet.

Next, consider how the original yarn is constructed. Is the design knit in a singles yarn or a plied yarn, a tape or a chainette? Is the yarn structure important to the integrity of the design, or is it incidental to the design? Was a woolen-spun yarn deliberately chosen to give a rustic effect? Are the tightly spun plies of the yarn essential so that the stitch pattern pops? Again, jot down your ideas to guide your choice of a substitute.

Finish up by considering the yarn's appearance. Are there color effects dyed into it? A self-striping yarn or a brightly colored hand-paint will look quite different than a machine-dyed solid yarn. Are there physical structures that affect the yarn's appearance, such as a contrasting binder thread or plies that each change color? How much does the appearance of the yarn affect the result? Is the yarn so unique that you can't imagine the design knit in something else?

The more you start to think about patterns in this way, the better you'll get at figuring out what kind of yarns will suit the pattern best. Is the design knit in a textured pattern? Put "stitch definition" on your list. Does the design use twisted stitches or cables? Write down "elasticity." Airy wraps require drape; socks and mittens will require durable yarns; shawls and cowls will give you much flexibility when it comes to yarn choice, since they tend not to get much direct wear. Are you knitting a bathing suit? Go with God, and make sure you use plant fiber for coolness—and some elastic or Lycra content so the moon doesn't come out early.

In time, these questions will become second nature as you study the pattern and the photographs that accompany it. Before you know it, you'll find yourself with very definite ideas about yarn choice and the substitution process will become easier and easier.

## DON'T FORGET THE ROMANCE

The "romance" section of a pattern—the introductory paragraph that describes the design—can be a terrific source of clues about the kind of yarn the designer chose and why. Sometimes the designer will come right out and say why one yarn or type of yarn was chosen. For example, "This baby sweater uses multidirectional knitting to show off a self-striping yarn," or "Mohair content gives this cowl a hazy, dreamy look." Sometimes the romance will give you subtler clues. Think about the adjectives used to describe the design. Words like "floaty," "swing," or "movement" suggest a yarn with drape. "Crisp" indicates good stitch definition, while "hazy" often means a yarn with a distinct halo. Add any important information to your worksheet.

## CAN I GOOGLE THAT?

If you aren't sure about the exact qualities your substitute yarn should have, don't forget about the excellent resource you have at your fingertips: the Internet. A quick search for the yarn or pattern name may uncover reviews, maybe even a blog post or knit-along that includes detailed information about yarn choice or the designer's thoughts when creating the pattern. The website Ravelry.com contains a staggering amount of information about yarns and patterns, including comments by knitters who have actually made the pattern and have ideas about their yarns' performance. Photos of others' finished garments can tell you a lot about potential substitute yarns. All this information will help guide your choices.

## QUANTITY OF YARN

We've already been using the worksheet to jot down some important information you'll need when substituting. Now take a look at the middle, where you'll see a place to write down the quantity of yarn you'll need. Don't simply write down the number of skeins the pattern calls for; yardage and weight can vary wildly from skein to skein and that will affect how much you will need to buy. Some patterns give you a total number of yards or meters, while others cite the number of skeins of the original yarn. If your pattern uses the latter, multiply the number of skeins required for your desired size by the yardage of each skein to get the total amount needed.

Example: My pattern states that I'll need fifteen balls of Happy Needles Yarn. Each skein of Happy Needles Yarn has 120 yards. I will need to purchase at least 1,800 yards of a substitute yarn of the same CYC category.

## QUANTITY QUERIES

There's nothing worse than running out of yarn when you are almost at the end of a project. Well, there is one thing worse: going to the yarn shop to buy another skein and finding that the yarn is sold out, discontinued, or that there's no more in the same dye lot. By purchasing an extra skein or two, you give yourself wiggle room just in case you need more yarn than the pattern estimate.

You may also run short of yarn for other reasons. If your row gauge is denser than the pattern's row gauge, you'll be working more rows than the designer did and will need more yarn to finish. If you're using a striping yarn and plan on manipulating the stripe colors (say, to make two sleeves with identical stripes), or are trying to minimize a pooling hand-paint, then you'll also require more yarn. If, for some reason, you make more than one or two swatches, you could also run a bit short at the end. (Professional designers include ample yardage for swatching in their yarn estimates, but it doesn't hurt to round up just in case.)

# 7

# SELECTING THE PERFECT SUBSTITUTE YARN

I t's the time we've all been waiting for: time to go yarn shopping. Whether you plan to make a new purchase at a knitting store or are "shopping" from your stash, it's always exciting to think about beginning a new project and finding the perfect yarn to knit it with. Grab your worksheet and let's get substituting!

## SHOPPING FOR SUBSTITUTE YARNS

The actual process of yarn selection has always reminded me of the college entrance exams that high school students take. These tests have two sections (or at least they did when I took them many years ago, using an abacus, stone tablets, and a stylus). The first section is multiple choice: you are given several alternative answers and you must select the correct one. In the second section, you are given a topic and you write an essay about it. The first section has one right answer for each question; the second section has many "right" answers, depending on who is writing it.

In yarn substitution, too, there are two "sections" or steps to the process. The first step is to determine what yarn category your pattern requires. When you begin looking for substitutes, you must limit yourself only to substitute yarns in the same category. If you remember only one thing about yarn substitution after reading this book, it's this one: STAY IN YOUR YARN'S LANE.

After you find the correct category (i.e., picked the correct answer from among the alternatives), you've arrived at the essay section. Just as there are a lot of right answers to an essay question, depending on the perspective of the author, so there are a lot of right answers to the question "What yarn in category X should I pick to make this project?" You'll be guided by certain general principles—the notes you've taken on your worksheet about the pattern—but you're probably going to find multiple yarns that satisfy these general criteria. You'll then look to personal factors—availability, cost, brand loyalty, and the like—to select one yarn from among the many choices. If the result pleases you and performs well, you've made the right choice for you.

You've already jotted down the original yarn's category, how much yarn you'll need, and other important factors to consider. Now take a look at each potential substitute yarn (sticking to the same category as the sample yarn) that is available to you. You may be able to immediately reject some of the possible choices in your category (for example, if you know you want a smooth, traditional yarn, no need to consider the highly textured novelty yarns on offer). For each yarn that remains, use one of the lines on the worksheet to take notes, starting with fiber content, put-up, and price.

**YARN:** *Spiffydoodles DK Merino*

**FIBER CONTENT:** *100% merino wool (not superwash)*

**PUT-UP:** *130 yards = 50 grams*

**PRICE PER SKEIN:** *$7.95*

**QUANTITY OF SKEINS:**

**TOTAL COST:**

**NOTES:**

## CALCULATING QUANTITY

Remember that yarns are packaged in skeins of varying weight and yardage. To figure out how many skeins you need of a substitute yarn, get out your calculator. Take the total number of yards you need for the pattern. Divide it by the number of yards per skein of the first potential substitute. Let's imagine you're making a baby sweater that requires 660 yards of yarn and using a substitute yarn that comes in 130-yard skeins:

660 yd ÷ 130 yds/skein = 5.076

Because we cannot buy partial skeins of yarn, in this case you would need to buy six skeins of this particular yarn to make the pattern.* Now calculate the total cost of the project for this particular yarn by multiplying the number of skeins you need by the price per skein:

6 skeins × $7.95 per skein = $47.70 total cost

Add this information to the appropriate box.

Now think about the needs of your pattern and your own preferences, and jot down the pros and cons of this specific yarn. For example, if you were planning to make a baby sweater, you might make notes about factors like machine washability, softness, and color selection.

Repeat this process for each of the potential substitute yarns. Let's suppose that you find five possible substitute yarns at your LYS:

---

* We've discussed the importance of picking up an extra skein or two as insurance, but to simplify things here, we are going to exclude the extra yarn when we calculate yardage and relative cost.

**YARN:** *Spiffydoodles DK Merino*

**FIBER CONTENT:** *100% merino wool (not superwash)*

**PUT-UP:** *130 yards = 50 grams*

**PRICE PER SKEIN:** *$7.95*

**QUANTITY OF SKEINS:** *6*

**TOTAL COST:** *$47.70*

**NOTES:** *Not machine washable, soft hand, cute colorways for baby*

**YARN:** *Magenta Mountain Baby*

**FIBER CONTENT:** *100% microfiber acrylic*

**PUT-UP:** *270 yards = 100 grams*

**PRICE PER SKEIN:** *$4.50*

**QUANTITY OF SKEINS:** *3*

**TOTAL COST:** *$13.50*

**NOTES:** *great price, machine wash/dry, not natural fiber, softer than I expected*

**YARN:** *Hepzibah's Hand-Paints Swdk*

FIBER CONTENT: *100% superwash merino wool*

PUT-UP: *140 yards = 50 grams*

PRICE PER SKEIN: *$15.95*

QUANTITY OF SKEINS: *5*

TOTAL COST: *$79.75*

NOTES: *machine washable, expensive!, gorgeous colorways*

---

**YARN:** *Exceptional Yarn co. basic DK*

FIBER CONTENT: *100% superwash wool*

PUT-UP: *390 yards = 150 grams*

PRICE PER SKEIN: *$16.25*

QUANTITY OF SKEINS: *2*

TOTAL COST: *$32.50*

NOTES: *Not quite as soft as merino, machine washable, lots of colors, very elastic and bouncy*

---

**YARN:** *Patty Jean's Cotton Deluxe*

FIBER CONTENT: *100% cotton*

PUT-UP: *137 yards = 50 grams*

PRICE PER SKEIN: *$6.50*

QUANTITY OF SKEINS: *5*

TOTAL COST: *$32.50*

NOTES: *super soft, machine washable, breathable, cool*

Now think about how your own preferences intersect with the qualities of each possible yarn choice.

- If cost is a key factor, you'll cross out the hand-painted yarn (which costs twice as much as most of the remaining options) and perhaps the second merino yarn (which costs about $10 per yard more than the rest). That leaves you with the super-economical choice of the synthetic yarn (a miraculous $12.50), the workhorse wool ($32.50), or the cotton (also $32.50).

- If you want the recipient to be able to machine wash the baby sweater, then you will immediately nix the first choice, which isn't machine washable. That leaves you with three machine-washable choices plus one machine-washable and dryable choice.

- If the baby lives in Arizona, the cotton may win because it's breathable and cool.

- Softness for a baby may guide your choice, and that factor might eliminate the fourth yarn (depending on its hand).

- Perhaps the gift is for a baby shower and the new mom's color theme is gray and pink. You may eliminate one of the choices because it doesn't come in the right shade of pink.

- Suppose the pattern features a textural stitch. The wool yarns will have the best elasticity, though the acrylic yarn will probably work well, too. The cotton might not work as well, given cotton's inherent lack of elasticity.

You can see how there isn't necessarily one right answer for the substitution question, just pros and cons, plus a whole lot of subjective factors. Put five knitters in a room and they may very well come up with five different substitutes—and all five may work perfectly well!

If you don't find a yarn that you like and that satisfies your most important criteria, then you may have to comparison shop elsewhere. Fortunately, even knitters who do not have access to a local yarn shop can comparison shop by looking at the wealth of choices online. Once you've got a particular yarn in mind, remember that you can always do an Internet search for it and read reviews and/or descriptions of its performance. That may help you avoid a bad choice or confirm your instinct.

# WHEN NOT TO SUBSTITUTE YARNS

Every once in a while, you'll come across a case in which the best yarn choice is the original yarn used in the pattern. This doesn't happen often, but remember that it can, and be ready to consider some of the scenarios where the original yarn just might be the ideal choice for your pattern. Sometimes it just so happens that the yarn used by the designer satisfies all your criteria and you have no reason to switch. In other cases, there is something unique about the yarn or the way it's used that make substitution more difficult. Here are some examples:

- **NOVELTY YARNS.** We spoke earlier about novelty yarns (page 61), which tend to be unique in appearance and construction. That uniqueness may make it difficult to find a substitute yarn that looks and acts like the original. Keep an open mind and swatch a lot!

- **DENIM YARN.** Several manufacturers make yarn from a dyed cotton similar to the denim used for blue jeans. These yarns are a bit different from other cotton yarns: like a pair of jeans, the yarn will shrink at the first laundering, and the color will fade the more it is worn and laundered. The effect can be very striking, but you'll need to keep the amount of shrinkage in mind when planning to substitute. If you use denim yarn as a substitute for a nondenim yarn, you will get substantial shrinkage after the first wash, which will significantly change the garment's dimensions. On the other hand, if you substitute nondenim yarn for a denim yarn, the lack of shrinkage will also change the garment's dimensions (and you'll lose the fascinating fading effect that comes with washing).

- **FELTING.** If you're going to felt your knitting, make sure you select a yarn that will, in fact, felt. Best to stick to an all-animal-fiber yarn (wool is particularly good), and make sure that the yarn hasn't been treated in such a way that it no longer will felt. Yarn that has been treated to be superwash will not felt. Some yarns that have been bleached before dyeing will also fail to felt. Research the line of yarn and the particular color you're looking at to make sure you don't end up with a felting disaster.

- **BESPOKE YARNS.** Patterns that use specially dyed or coordinating yarns may also be tricky. A manufacturer may use some standard colors for different weights or lines of yarn, so that you can purchase a skein of worsted-weight wool and a skein of fingering-weight mohair that were dyed in the same exact color. Sometimes dyers will create a solid yarn that exactly matches one of the colors in a multicolor yarn. It could be tough to find substitute yarns that match color as well.

## TWO IS NOT ALWAYS GREATER THAN ONE

Occasionally a pattern will call for the knitter to use two yarns held together. If you're substituting in this scenario, start by figuring out why the designer has chosen to double-strand yarn. If the designer is using two different yarns to achieve an aesthetic effect, you'll have to do a separate substitution analysis for each component yarn. Suppose the designer is using one strand of a hand-painted yarn and one strand of a mohair/silk blend to achieve a dreamy and somewhat muted multicolor look. To get the same look while substituting, you'll want to look for one hand-painted yarn and one mohair/silk (or other hazy) yarn.

Sometimes a designer will combine two strands of the same yarn to achieve a thicker gauge (or someone will suggest to you that you double-strand even though the designer has not). Proceed very carefully. It's difficult to predict how yarns will perform when they are double-stranded, notwithstanding any general rules you've heard. (The one I've heard most often is that double-stranding a yarn will give you a gauge that is one to two categories larger than the category of the yarn used by itself, but please take this with a very large grain of salt.)

Double-stranded yarns frequently trap air as the strands twist around each other; the texture or slipperiness of the yarn can also affect how well the individual strands stick together. This may result in an unusual knitted fabric that feels bulky, thick, and inflexible. You must swatch a lot, playing with various needle sizes, and you may find that the fabric you like best is knit at a different gauge than the one you're looking to substitute.

The moral of the story: tread carefully when double-stranding yarn, and don't assume that any specific combination of yarns will get the gauge and fabric you're looking for unless you try them out yourself first.

## PRACTICE, PRACTICE, THEN GO FORTH AND CONQUER!

The knack of substituting yarns is not a magical gift that fairy godmothers bestow upon some people, but not others, at birth. It's a skill like any other that may seem hard at first but becomes easier the more practice you have. You now have the basic information you need to substitute yarns. Use the patterns in the section that follows to practice your new skills.

III
# PATTERNS
# FOR
# PRACTICING

# PUTTING THEORY INTO PRACTICE

The only way to improve your skills at yarn substitution is to practice them. The ten patterns that follow are an easy and fun way to start. Each pattern highlights one yarn substitution principle, explained in the pattern introduction. You'll also find swatches of three possible substitute yarns. I've graded each swatch with a red, yellow, or green symbol: green for a yarn which would be a good substitute for the pattern, red for a yarn that is unsuitable for the project, and yellow meaning proceed with caution. Keep in mind that a yarn may not be a good fit for a specific pattern, but that does not mean it isn't a good yarn—you just need to find the project that's right for it.

UNSUITABLE     PROCEED WITH     GOOD
               CAUTION          SUBSTITUTE

I've matched the categories for you—each substitute yarn is the same category number as the yarn used in the original pattern (except for the patterns written for multiple gauges), so you can focus on other factors. The one thing I cannot factor in is your subjective preferences or your motivation for substituting—you'll have to do that part yourself!

# Blissful Beanie

Ribbing gives this classic watch-style cap stretch and holds it close to your head to keep you warm; a classic twisted-stitch pattern adds a bit of flair. A yarn with good **stitch definition**, like the supersoft worsted-spun wool used in the original, makes the pattern pop so that each individual stitch can be seen and appreciated.

## SKILL LEVEL

**EASY**

## FINISHED MEASUREMENTS

Head circumference (stretches to fit):
18–20 (20–22, 22–23)"/46–51 (51–56, 56–58.5)cm

Length: 8 (8½, 9)"/20.5 (21.5, 23)cm

## SIZING

To fit Teen/Adult Small (Adult Medium, Adult Large)

## MATERIALS AND TOOLS

Stonehedge Fiber Mill Shepherd's Wool Worsted (100% wool; 4oz/113g = 250yd/229m): 1 skein, color Turquoise—approx 150yd/137m of worsted weight yarn

Knitting needles:

4.5mm (size 7 US) 16"/40cm circular needle or size to obtain gauge

Set of four 4.5mm (size 7 US) double-pointed needles or second circular needle

4mm (size 6 US) 16"/40cm circular needle (or one size smaller)

Stitch marker

Tapestry needle

## GAUGE

22 sts/30 rnds = 4"/10cm over pattern stitch using larger needle

**NOTE:** Always take time to check your gauge.

## SPECIAL ABBREVIATIONS

RT (right twist)

Knit 2 sts tog, but do not drop old sts from needle; knit first st again dropping old sts from needle.

Rib and Twist Pattern:

(over a multiple of 8 sts)

RND 1: *RT, p2, k2, p2; rep from * to end.

RNDS 2–5: *K2, p2; rep from * to end.

RND 6: *K2, p2, RT, p2; rep from * to end.

RNDS 7–10: *K2, p2; rep from * to end.

Rep Rnds 1–10 for Rib and Twist patt.

## INSTRUCTIONS

Border:

Using smaller needle, CO 88 (96, 104) sts. Join, being careful not to twist sts, and place marker for beg of rnd.

RIB RND: *K2, p2; rep from * to end of rnd.

Rep rib rnd until hat measures 1¼"/3cm from beg.

Change to larger needle and work rib rnd once more.

Beanie:

Work in Rib and Twist patt until cap measures 7 (7½, 8)"/17.5 (19, 20.25)cm from beg, ending with a Rnd 2.

## Crown shaping:

**NOTE:** Change to double-pointed needles or add 2nd circular needle when there are too few stitches to fit comfortably on one circular needle.

**Next rnd:** *K2, p2tog; rep from * to end of rnd—66 (72, 78) sts.

**Next 2 rnds:** *K2, p1; rep from * to end of rnd.

**Next rnd:** *K2, p1, RT, p1; rep from * to end of rnd.

**Next rnd:** *K2, p1; rep from * to end of rnd.

**Next rnd:** *K2tog, p1; rep from * to end of rnd—44 (48, 52) sts.

**Next 2 rnds:** *K1, p1; rep from * to end of rnd.

**Next rnd:** *K2tog; rep from * to end of rnd—22 (24, 26) sts.

Knit 1 rnd.

**Next rnd:** *K2tog; rep from * to end of rnd—11 (12, 13) sts.

**Next rnd:** [K2tog] 5 (6, 6) times, k1 (0, 1)—6 (6, 7) sts.

Break off yarn, leaving a long tail. Thread tail through rem sts to close.

## FINISHING:

Weave in ends and steam to block.

## SUBSTITUTE YARN SWATCH

## STATS

## YES / **NO** / MAYBE SO

YARN A

### BLUE SKY FIBERS ORGANIC WORSTED COTTON

**Fiber content:** 100% organic cotton

**Put-up:** 100g = 150yd/137m

**Price per skein\*:** $14.60

**Number of skeins:** 1

**Total cost:** $14.60

\*I've used MSRP at the time of this writing; prices are subject to change, but you will be able to get a general sense of comparative price by using these numbers.

The original yarn was chosen for its crisp stitch definition, softness, and warmth. Its worsted construction gives it elasticity, which is also important for a ribbing-based pattern. Substitute A is plush and supersoft, but its cotton fiber will not have the same elasticity as a wool yarn, causing the ribbing to sag over time. Another reason I'd use this yarn for a different project: it is made by plying two softly spun singles together; this relatively loose construction makes it less durable and thus subject to pilling.

YARN B

### MALABRIGO WORSTED

**Fiber content:** 100% merino wool

**Put-up:** 100g = 210yd/192m

**Price per skein:** $12

**Number of skeins:** 1

**Total cost:** $12

Substitute B is a lovely hand-painted yarn made of 100 percent wool. This is a great substitute yarn, as long as you select a colorway with care. A colorway with many bright colors may pool, drawing attention away from the beauty of the stitch pattern; a colorway that is more muted will allow the twisted rib pattern to be clearly visible. The colorway used here is a bit too dark to allow the stitch pattern to shine; you'll have to decide if that's a dealbreaker.

YARN C

### PREMIER® YARNS DEBORAH NORVILLE COLLECTION™ ALPACA DANCE™

**Fiber content:** 75% acrylic/ 25% alpaca

**Put-up:** 100g = 371yd/339m

**Price per skein:** $6.49

**Number of skeins:** 1

**Total cost:** $6.49

Substitute C is an acrylic/alpaca blend. While alpaca doesn't have a lot of elasticity, the acrylic content will compensate for that. Note that the yarn has a subtle haze (a quality of many alpaca yarns). Sometimes a haze is pronounced enough to detract from a stitch pattern. I think this particular yarn, especially when a light color is used, gives a very attractive muted effect.

# Sweet Valley Cardigan

SUBSTITUTION PRINCIPLE: DRAPE
• PLANT FIBERS DRAPE WELL
• TEXTURE AND FUZZ MAY CREATE CLING
• TAPES AND RIBBONS TEND TO DRAPE

Some patterns require a yarn with **drape**, and the Sweet Valley Cardigan, with its softly flowing collar, is one of them. Drape can be created by knitting stitches loosely, by the inherent qualities of the fiber, or by both. In this case, the natural softness and inelasticity in this luscious baby alpaca yarn create the drape in this versatile, easy-to-wear cardigan.

**SKILL LEVEL**

EASY

**FINISHED MEASUREMENTS**

Finished chest: 36 (40, 44, 48, 52)"/91.5 (101.5, 112, 122, 132)cm

Finished Length: 21½ (22, 23, 24, 25½)"/54.5 (56, 58.5, 61, 65)cm

**SIZING**

To fit Women's Small (Medium, Large, X-Large, 1X)

**MATERIALS AND TOOLS**

Valley Yarns® Sunderland (100% baby alpaca; 1.76oz/50g = 109yd/100m): 11 (11, 12, 13, 14) skeins, color Plum—approx 1150 (1200, 1300, 1400, 1520yd/1052 (1097, 1189, 1280, 1389)m of DK weight yarn

Knitting needles: 4mm (size 6 US) or size to obtain gauge

Size G-6 (4mm) crochet hook

Stitch markers

Tapestry needle

**GAUGE**

19 sts/28 rows = 4"/10cm over St st

**NOTE:** Always take time to check your gauge.

## INSTRUCTIONS

### Back:

CO 90 (100, 110, 120, 130) sts.

Work in St st until piece measures 14 (14, 14½, 14½, 15)"/35.5 (35.5, 37, 37, 38) cm, ending with a WS row.

### Armhole shaping:

BO 6 sts at beg of next 2 rows—78 (88, 98, 108, 118) sts.

Dec 1 st at each end of next 0 (0, 0, 2, 3) RS rows —78 (88, 98, 104, 112) sts.

### Begin raglan shaping:

**Next row (RS):** K2, ssk, k to last 4 sts, k2tog, k2—2 sts dec.

**Next row:** Purl.

Rep these 2 rows, dec 2 sts every RS row, until 26 (32, 38, 40, 44) sts rem.

BO all sts loosely knitwise.

### Right Front:

CO 92 (94, 96, 104, 106) sts.

Work in St st until piece measures 14 (14, 14½, 14½, 15)"/35.5 (35.5, 37, 37, 38) cm, ending with a WS row.

### Armhole shaping:

BO 6 sts at beg of next WS row— 86 (88, 90, 98, 100) sts.

Dec 1 st at end of next 0 (0, 0, 2, 3) RS rows—86 (88, 90, 96, 97) sts.

### Begin raglan shaping:

**Next row:** K to last 4 sts, k2tog, k2—1 st dec.

**Next row:** Purl.

Rep these 2 rows, dec 1 st at end of every RS row, until 60 (60, 60, 64, 63) sts rem. BO all sts loosely knitwise.

## Left Front:

CO 92 (94, 96, 104, 106) sts.

Work in St st until piece measures 14 (14, 14½, 14½, 15)"/35.5 (35.5, 37, 37, 38) cm, ending with a WS row.

## Armhole shaping:

BO 6 sts at beg of next RS row—86 (88, 90, 98, 100) sts.

Dec 1 st at beg of next 0 (0, 0, 2, 3) RS rows—86 (88, 90, 96, 97) sts rem.

## Begin Raglan Shaping:

NEXT ROW (RS): K2, ssk, k to end.

NEXT ROW (WS): Purl.

Rep these 2 rows, dec 1 st at beg of every RS row, until 60 (60, 60, 64, 63) sts rem. BO all sts loosely knitwise.

## Sleeve (make 2):

CO 42 (46, 50, 50, 50) sts.

Work 5 rows in St st, beg wwith a WS row.

INC ROW (RS): K2, M1R, k to last 2 sts, M1L, k2.

NEXT ROW (WS): Purl.

Cont in St st, rep inc row every 8th (8th, 6th, 6th, 4th) row until there are 72, (76, 80, 92, 100) sts. Work even until sleeve measures 18"/46cm from beg edge, ending with a WS row.

BO 6 (6, 6, 6, 6) sts at beg of next 2 rows—60 (64, 68, 80, 88) sts.

Dec 1 st each end of the next 0 (0, 0, 2, 3) RS rows—60 (64, 68, 76, 85) sts.

## Begin raglan decreases:

NEXT ROW (RS): K2, ssk, knit across to last 4 sts, k2tog, k2—2 sts dec.

NEXT ROW: Purl.

Rep last 2 rows until 8 (8, 8, 12, 17) sts rem. Bind off loosely knitwise. Weave in ends.

**FINISHING:**

Block all pieces to measurements. Sew sleeves to back along raglan shaping.

Sew fronts to sleeves along raglan shaping. Sew sleeve and side seams.

With RS facing, join yarn to lower right front edge. Work 1 row single crochet along right center front, around neck, and down left center front. Fasten off.

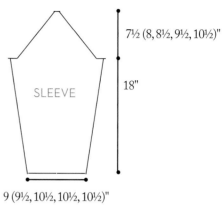

7½ (8, 8½, 9½, 10½)"

18"

SLEEVE

9 (9½, 10½, 10½, 10½)"

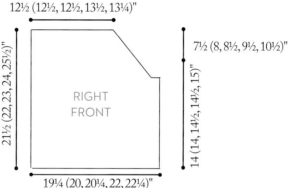

12½ (12½, 12½, 13½, 13¼)"

21½ (22, 23, 24, 25½)"

RIGHT FRONT

7½ (8, 8½, 9½, 10½)"

14 (14, 14½, 14½, 15)"

19¼ (20, 20¼, 22, 22¼)"

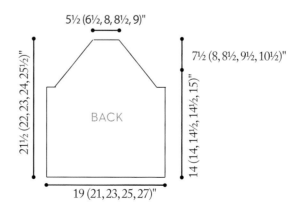

5½ (6½, 8, 8½, 9)"

21½ (22, 23, 24, 25½)"

BACK

7½ (8, 8½, 9½, 10½)"

14 (14, 14½, 14½, 15)"

19 (21, 23, 25, 27)"

| SUBSTITUTE YARN SWATCH | STATS | YES / **NO** / MAYBE SO |
|---|---|---|

YARN A

**UNIVERSAL YARN BAMBOO POP**

**Fiber content:** 50% cotton/50% bamboo

**Put-up:** 100g = 292yd/267m

**Price per skein:** $9.50

**Number of skeins:** 4

**Total cost:** $38

The flowing fronts and relaxed style of the Sweet Valley Cardigan call for a yarn with drape, like the 100 percent alpaca yarn used for the original. Substitute A is knit with a cotton/bamboo blend, a good fiber choice given the natural tendency of bamboo fiber to drape. I also like the plied construction of this yarn, which is helpful for ensuring that drape doesn't turn into droop.

YARN B

**WEST YORKSHIRE SPINNERS FLEECE JACOB DK**

**Fiber content:** 100% British Jacob wool

**Put-up:** 100g = 253yd/231m

**Price per skein:** $9.50

**Number of skeins:** 5

**Total cost:** $47.50

Substitute B is an all-wool yarn in a heritage breed. Jacob sheep have fleeces that range in softness; while this yarn has a nice hand, Jacob wool has bounce and elasticity rather than drape. I would save this yarn for a pattern with cables or textured stitches instead, since the knitted fabric just isn't flowing enough for this pattern.

YARN C

**MANOS SILK BLEND**

**Fiber content:** 70% wool/ 30% silk

**Put-up:** 50g = 150yd/135m

**Price per skein:** $16

**Number of skeins:** 8

**Total cost:** $128

Substitute C is a glorious hand-painted blend of wool and silk. I've given this yarn a yellow symbol for a few reasons. While the yarn's 30 percent silk will give the fabric some drape, you'll have to judge whether you like the resulting fabric for this project given that the silk constitutes only about a third of the fibers in the yarn. The yarn's singles construction may not wear as well as a plied yarn, so you may see some abrading on elbows and other high-wear places. As with any hand-painted yarn, you'll also want to think long and hard about colorway selection. Make sure you're comfortable with the brightness of the colorway and keep an eye out for pooling.

# Nina's Hanska

SUBSTITUTION PRINCIPLE: **ELASTICITY**
- WOOL IS MOST ELASTIC
- PLIED WOOL & CHAINETTES BUILD IN SPRING
- TEST A STRAND BY TUGGING GENTLY

**Elasticity**, or the ability of a yarn to stretch and bounce back, is especially important when knitting cables or ribbing. These charming wristers have both, so the elasticity of the wool in this yarn is essential to keep cables looking sharp and ribbing tight. Wristers don't take long to knit and are a great gift. Grab some single skeins of your favorite yarn and play!

## SKILL LEVEL

**INTERMEDIATE**

## FINISHED MEASUREMENTS

Hand circumference: 6 (7½)" 15 (19)cm

Length: 7½"/19cm

## SIZING

To fit S–M: 6½–8" (17–20)cm;  M–L: 8–9½" (20–24)cm (ribbing creates some flexibility in fit)

## MATERIALS AND TOOLS

Black Bunny Fibers Devon (70% merino wool/20% baby alpaca/10% silk; 3½oz/100g = 240yd/214m): 1 skein, color Suck It Up Buttercup—approx 145 (165)yd/133 (151)m of DK weight yarn

Knitting needles: Two 3.75mm (size 5 US) 24"/60cm circular needles or size to obtain gauge

Stitch markers

Cable needle

Scrap yarn or stitch holder

Tapestry needle

## GAUGE

22 sts/30 rnds = 4"/10cm over St st

**NOTE:** Always take time to check your gauge.

## SPECIAL ABBREVIATIONS

1/4LC (left-crossing cable):

Slip next st from left-hand needle to cable needle and hold to front, k4 from left-hand needle, k1 from cable needle.

1/4RC (right-crossing cable):

Slip 4 sts from left-hand needle to cable needle and hold to back, k1 from left-hand needle, k4 from cable needle.

M1L (make 1 left]:

Pick up bar in between two sts by inserting left-hand needle from front to back. Knit into back of this st to increase 1 st. New st will lean to left.

M1R (make 1 right]:

Pick up bar in between two sts by inserting left-hand needle from back to front. Knit into front of this st to increase 1 st. New st will lean to right.

Slipped- Stitch Cable Pattern:

(multiple of 11 sts)

**Rnds 1 and 2:** P3, sl 1, k4, p3.

**Rnd 3:** P3, 1/4 LC, p3.

**Rnds 4–6:** P3, k5, p3.

**Rnds 7 and 8:** P3, k4, sl 1, p3.

**Rnd 9:** P3, 1/4 RC, p3.

**Rnds 10–12:** P3, k5, p3.

Rep Rnds 1–12 for Slipped St Cable patt.

## INSTRUCTIONS

Using the 2 circular method, CO 37 (45) sts, with 19 (23) sts on first (front) needle, and 18 (22) sts on second (back) needle. Join, being careful not to twist sts.

## Cuff:

### Rnd 1:

**Needle 1:** K0 (2), p2, k2, place marker (pm), p3, k5, p3, pm, k2, p2, k0 (2).

**Needle 2:** *K2, p2, rep from * to last 2 sts, k2.

### Rnd 2:

**Needle 1:** K0 (2), p2, k2, sl m, p to marker, sl m, k2, p2, k0 (2).

**Needle 2:** K the knit sts and p the purl sts.

Rep rnds Rnds 1 and 2 once more—4 rnds worked.

## Begin cable pattern

### Rnd 5:

**Needle 1:** K0 (2), p2, sl m, work Rnd 1 of Slipped St Cable patt, sl m, k2, p2, k0 (2).

**Needle 2:** K the knit sts and p the purl sts.

**Rnd 6:** K the knit sts and p the purl sts, maintaining Slipped St Cable patt on Needle 1 by working next rnd between markers.

Cont in this manner, working each sequential row of Slipped St cable patt between markers until cuff measures 2"/5cm from beg.

### Next rnd:

**Needle 1:** K to marker, work next row of Slipped St Cable patt, k to end of needle.

**Needle 2:** Knit.

Rep this rnd until cuff measures 1"/2.5cm from end of rib, or desired length to beg of thumb gusset.

## Begin thumb gusset:

### Left hand

### Next rnd:

**Needle 1:** K1, pm, M1L, k1, M1R, pm, cont in patt as established to end of this needle.

**Needle 2:** Knit.

### Rnd 2:

**Needle 1:** Cont in patt as established.

**Needle 2:** Knit.

### Rnd 3:

**Needle 1:** K1, sl m, M1L, k to marker, M1R, sl m, cont in patt as established to end of this needle.

**Needle 2:** Knit.

Rep Rnds 2 and 3 until there are 15 (17) sts between gusset markers, then work Rnd 2 once more.

Place thumb sts (sts between markers) on scrap yarn or stitch holder.

### Right Hand

### Next rnd:

**Needle 1:** Work in patt as established to last 2 sts on this needle, pm, M1L, k1, M1R, pm, k1.

**Needle 2:** Knit.

### Rnd 2:

**Needle 1:** Cont in patt as established.

**Needle 2:** Knit.

### Rnd 3:

**Needle 1:** Work in patt as established to marker, M1L, k1, M1R, pm, k1.

**Needle 2:** Knit.

Rep Rnds 2 and 3 until there are 15 (17) sts between gusset markers, then work Rnd 2 once more.

Place thumb sts (sts bet markers) on scrap yarn or stitch holder.

### Both wristers:

**Next rnd:** Work in patt as established, casting on 2 sts over gap left by thumb sts.

Cont in patt as established until wrister is 1¾ (2¼)"/4 (6)cm from last gusset rnd, ending with a Rnd 10 or 16.

Knit 1 rnd, dec 1 st on each needle.

**Next rnd:** *K2, p2, rep from * to end of rnd.

Rep this rnd 3 three times more, then BO all sts in pattern.

### Thumb:

Transfer sts from holder or scrap yarn to 2 circular needles dividing sts evenly.

Knit 1 rnd, picking up 2 sts in the cast-on edge.

Knit every rnd until thumb measures 1"/2.5cm, dec 1 st on last rnd.

Work in k1, p1 rib for 4 rnds. BO all sts in pattern.

### FINISHING:

Weave in ends and steam block.

| SUBSTITUTE YARN SWATCH | STATS | YES / **NO** / MAYBE SO |
|---|---|---|

YARN A

**BLACK BUNNY FIBERS PENFIELD**

**Fiber content:** 100% hand-painted merino wool

**Put-up:** 100g = 275yd/251m

**Price per skein:** $24

**Number of skeins:** 1

**Total cost:** $24

The lovely cabled pattern that is the focal point of these wristers begs for a yarn with elasticity, like the original yarn, which is mostly merino wool with a plied construction. Look for a yarn that has similar spring and bounce for best results. Substitute A is all merino wool—a naturally elastic fiber—and is made with a chainette construction, which will enhance elasticity. It would be a great substitute for this pattern.

YARN B

**PATTONS® SILK BAMBOO™**

**Fiber content:** 70% viscose from bamboo/30% silk

**Put-up:** 65g = 102yd/93m

**Price per skein:** $6.99

**Number of skeins:** 2

**Total cost:** $13.98

Substitute B is a bamboo/silk blend, which has lovely drape and sheen, but is not elastic and is very soft and slick. This blend will feel incredibly good next to your skin but simply doesn't have the memory necessary for a pattern that is intended to fit closely and stay in place. A shawl or cowl would be a much better use for these lusciously soft fibers.

YARN C

**BERNAT® SOFTEE® BABY™**

Fiber content: 100% acrylic

Put-up: 140g = 362yd/331m

Price per skein: $5.49

Number of skeins: 1

Total cost: $5.49

Substitute C is a great choice if budget is a prime concern: its all-acrylic blend should hold its shape well. All-synthetic yarns do not breathe, so this yarn may make your hands a bit clammy, which is why I've graded it yellow.

# Clancy Capelet

I've always been fascinated with yarns that have interesting **color effects,** and this capelet was designed to showcase them. Working in the round allows stripes to stack in varying widths. Ribbing at the neck and a gently scalloped lace border add visual interest. Whether you opt for stripes, gradients, or other colorful effects, this capelet gives you the cozy joy of a warm embrace.

## SKILL LEVEL

INTERMEDIATE

## FINISHED MEASUREMENTS

Circumference at lower edge: Approx 44 (48, 52)"/112 (122, 132)cm

Neck circumference: 24 (26, 28)"/61 (66, 71)cm

Length: 18 (19, 20)"/46 (48, 51)cm

## SIZING

To fit Women's Small (Medium, Large)

## MATERIALS AND TOOLS

Universal Yarns Poems Silk (75% wool, 25% silk; 1.75oz/50g = 109yd/100m): 7 (9, 12) skeins, color 800—approx 700 (900, 1175)yd/640 (823, 1074)m of worsted-weight yarn

Knitting needles: 5mm (size 8 US) 24"/60cm circular needle or size to obtain gauge

Set of double-pointed needles or second circular needle in same size as above

Stitch marker

Tapestry needle

## GAUGE

18 sts/28 rnds = 4"/10cm over St st, before blocking

**NOTE:** Always take time to check your gauge.

## SPECIAL ABBREVIATIONS

S2KP (slip 2 sts, knit 1, pass slipped sts over):

Slip 2 sts knitwise to right-hand needle as if to knit 2 together, knit next st, then pass both slipped sts together over the knit st.

## INSTRUCTIONS

Note: Capelet is knit from lower edge to neck.

Change to double-pointed needles or add 2nd circular needle when there are too few stitches to fit comfortably on one circular needle.

Border:

Using circular needle, CO 198 (216, 234) sts. Join, being careful not to twist sts, and place marker for beg of rnd.

RND 1: Purl.

RND 2: [P3, k11, p3, k1] 11 (12, 13) times around.

RND 3: *[Yo, ssk] twice, k9, [k2tog, yo] twice, k1; rep from * around.

RND 4: [P4, k9, p4, k1] 11 (12, 13) times around.

RND 5: *K1, [yo, ssk] twice, k7, [k2tog, yo] twice, k2; rep from * around.

RND 6: [K2, p3, k7, p3, k3] 11 (12, 13) times around.

RND 7: *K2, [yo, ssk] twice, k2, knit into st 3 rnds below and pull up a loop [yo, knit into same st 3 rnds below and pull up a loop] twice, drop st from left-hand needle—5 bobble sts, k2, [k2tog, yo] twice, k3; rep from * around—11 (12, 13) bobbles begun.

RND 8: [K2, p4, k2, k5 bobble sts, k2, p4, k3] 11 (12, 13) times around.

RND 9: *K3, [yo, ssk] twice, k1, k5 bobble sts tog, k1, [k2tog, yo] twice, k4; rep from * around.

RND 10: [K4, p9, k4] 11 (12, 13) times around.

RND 11: *K4, [yo, ssk] twice, k1, [k2tog, yo] twice, k5; rep from * around.

RND 12: [K4, p4, k1, p4, k5] 11 (12, 13) times around.

RND 13: [K5, yo, ssk, yo, S2KP, yo, k2tog, yo, k6] 11 (12, 13) times around.

RND 14: [K6, p5, k7] 11 (12, 13) times around.

**Rnd 15:** [K6, yo, ssk, p1, k2tog, yo, k7] 11 (12, 13) times around.

**Rnd 16:** [K6, p5, k7] 11 (12, 13) times around.

**Rnd 17:** [K7, yo, S2KP, yo, k8] 11 (12, 13) times around.

Capelet:

Work in St st (knit every rnd) until piece measures 6"/15cm from beg.

Begin shaping:

**Dec rnd:** *K16, k2tog, rep from * around—187 (204, 221) sts.

Work even until piece measures 7 1/2 (8, 9)"/19 (20, 23)cm from beg.

**Dec rnd:** *K15, k2tog, rep from * around—176 (192, 208) sts.

Work even until piece measures 9 (9 1/2, 10½)"/23 (24, 27)cm from beg.

**Dec rnd:** *K14, k2tog, rep from * around—165 (180, 195) sts.

Work even until piece measures 12 (12 1/2, 13½)"/30 (32, 34)cm from cast-on edge.

**Dec rnd:** *K13, k2tog, rep from * around—154 (168, 182) sts.

Knit 3 rnds, decreasing 4 (3, 2) sts evenly across last round—150 (165, 180) sts.

**Next rnd:** *K3, p2, rep from * around for k3, p2 rib.

Work in k3, p2 rib until piece measures 15 (15½, 16½)"/38 (39, 42)cm from beg.

**Next rnd:** *K2tog, k1, p2, rep from * around—120 (132, 144) sts.

**Next rnd:** *K2, p2, rep from * around for k2, p2 rib.

Work in k2, p2 rib until piece measures 18 (19, 20)"/46 (48, 51)cm from beg, or desired length.

BO in patt. Weave in ends and block as desired, pinning out lace edging to desired shape.

YARN A

### CASCADE YARNS® 220 SUPERWASH® EFFECTS

**Fiber content:** 100% superwash wool

**Put-up:** 100g = 220yd/201m

**Price per skein:** $14.50

**Number of skeins:** 4

**Total cost:** $58

This capelet is the perfect canvas for playing with color effects. The self-striping yarn used in the sample adds color and enhances the circular shape of the capelet. A set of mini-skeins would create a similar effect, as would a gradient (the colors change less abruptly in a gradient). Color effects aren't limited to stripes, though. Substitute A has a speckled effect that is less regular than stripes, with darker areas of specks and splatter in randomized intervals. I've graded it green because the yarn is interesting enough to add some variety to the stockinette areas but is muted enough to show off the lace edging.

YARN B

### LORNA'S LACES SHEPHERD WORSTED

**Fiber content:** 100% superwash wool

**Put-up:** 100g = 225yd/206m

**Price per skein:** $24

**Number of skeins:** 4

**Total cost:** $96

Substitute B is a plush all-wool hand-paint, but its vivid mixture of colors creates a very bright effect and has the potential to pool. (The colors also may overwhelm the lacy edging.) You'll have to play with this one to see if you like the finished effect, and you may want to alternate two different skeins as you go to minimize pooling—hence the yellow grade.

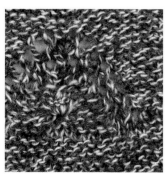

YARN C

### PATTONS® CLASSIC WOOL WORSTED™

**Fiber content:** 100% wool

**Put-up:** 100g = 223yd/206m

**Price per skein:** $6.99

**Number of skeins:** 4

**Total cost:** $27.96

The last yarn is a marled yarn, with two different-colored plies. I've graded it red because the color effects of the yarn drown out the stitchwork in the lace edging. Marled yarns can vary from dramatic to subtle depending on the value and color differences between the two plies. The value differences in this colorway are too strong for the lace pattern, but would be fetching in a ribbed or stockinette pattern.

# Stacy's Mom's Cowl

## UNUSUAL YARN CONSTRUCTION

SUBSTITUTION PRINCIPLE: UNUSUAL
YARN CONSTRUCTION
• MAY NOT BE STURDY
• DETRACTS FROM COMPLICATED PATTERNS
• HARD TO PREDICT FINISHED LOOK

Cowls, like this quick-knitting one, are the perfect way to take a new yarn for a test drive. That's why I've included this multigauge pattern: just swatch, measure your gauge, and use the corresponding stitch numbers to cast on. Be sure to play around with yarns with an **unusual construction**. This super-bulky beauty is made of a softly twisted wool roving wrapped with a thin binder thread. The black binder thread contrasts with the colorful wool it wraps, giving the knit fabric a stained-glass effect.

### SKILL LEVEL

**EASY**

### FINISHED MEASUREMENTS

Circumference: 23"/58cm

Height: 9½"/24cm

### MATERIALS AND TOOLS

Malabrigo Caracol (100% wool;
5.3oz/150g = 90yd/87m): 1 skein, color
639 Rose—approx 90yd/87m of super-
bulky weight yarn

Knitting needles: 9mm (size 13 US)
16"/40cm circular needle or size to
obtain gauge (see chart at right)

Stitch marker

Tapestry needle

### GAUGE

Gauge for sample pattern (category 6 yarn)

10 sts/16 rnds = 4"/10cm over Welted Rib
patt.

Calculate gauge for other categories at
right.

### YARDAGE/NEEDLE REQUIREMENTS

| YARN CAT. | YARDAGE (APPROX YDS) | APPROX NEEDLE SIZE (MM/US) |
|---|---|---|
| 1 | 325 | 3/3 |
| 2 | 275 | 3.75/5 |
| 3 | 225 | 4.5/7 |
| 4 | 175 | 5.5/9 |
| 5 | 120 | 9/13 |

## PATTERN STITCH

Welted Rib Pattern:

(multiple of 5 sts)

RNDS 1–3: *K3, p2, rep from * to end of rnd.

RNDS 4 AND 5: Purl.

Rep Rnds 1–5 for welted rib patt.

## INSTRUCTIONS

Knit a gauge swatch in Welted Rib patt and write the number of stitches per 1"/2.5cm in the first blank below:

_____ (sts/in) × 23"/58cm (desired circumference) = _____. Round this total to the nearest multiple of 5. This is the number of stitches to cast on.

CO required number of sts as calculated above. Join, being careful not to twist sts, and place marker for beg of rnd.

Knit 1 rnd; purl 1 rnd.

Work in Welted Rib patt until cowl measures 9"/23cm or desired length.

Purl 1 rnd; knit 1 rnd.

BO all sts knitwise. Weave in loose ends and block as desired.

YARN A

### BERGERE DE FRANCE TOISON

**Fiber content:** 75% acrylic/20% wool/3% polyamide

**Put-up:** 100g = 76yd/70m

**Price per skein:** $4.89

**Number of skeins:** 2

**Total cost:** $9.78

This cowl pattern is incredibly versatile and will work well with all sorts of yarns. It's hard to imagine a "wrong" choice—just many *different* choices. The original yarn is a multicolored roving wrapped with a thin black binder, a unique combination that creates a stained-glass effect. Substitute A is a bouclé yarn, with the characteristic loops; this yarn also has a slightly brushed finish that creates a haze. The overall look is warm and cozy, reminiscent of a fuzzy teddy bear.

YARN B

### COLINETTE GIOTTO

**Fiber content:** 50% cotton/40% rayon/10% nylon

**Put-up:** 100g = 156yd/143m

**Price per skein:** $29.99

**Number of skeins:** 1

**Total cost:** $29.99

Substitute B is a lush tape in a cotton/rayon blend. The two fibers give different textures (the rayon's shine makes the colors pop). You'll get a very different look with this yarn. Unlike the other two swatches, this tape is slick rather than plump. The cowl will be more loose and open, perfect for multiseason wear.

YARN C

### SIRDAR PLUSHTWEED

**Fiber content:** 100% polyester

**Put-up:** 100100g = 72yd/66m

**Price per skein:** $8.99

**Number of skeins:** 2

**Total cost:** $17.98

Substitute C takes the cowl in yet another direction. This plush velourlike yarn has a thick, slinky texture. Its subtle multicolored fibers give it an almost marbled look. There really aren't any wrong answers with this one; just plug in your gauge and have fun.

# Miz Brown's Mittens

Yarn choice is important when working **stranded knitting** patterns. Traditionally, stranded knitting is done with rustic yarns that are spun woolen-style. These yarns have a "sticky" feel and may seem a bit rougher in the ball if you're used to more processed yarns, but their tendency to mesh together creates a cohesive fabric that fills in any spaces left by switching from one yarn color to the next (it also helps keep floats—the sections of unused yarn that run across the back of a stranded piece—in place). These mittens are knit in Rauma Finullgarn, a Norwegian wool with a crunchy texture and long tradition of being used for stranded knitting.

## SKILL LEVEL

INTERMEDIATE

## FINISHED MEASUREMENTS

Hand circumference: 7¼ (8½)"/18.5 (22)cm

Length: 8¾ (9¼ )"/22.5 (23.5)cm

## SIZING

To fit Women's Small/Medium (Medium/Large)

## MATERIALS AND TOOLS

Rauma Finullgarn (100% wool; 1.76oz/50g = 191yd/175m): (A) 1 (2) skeins, color 404 (light grey)—approx 160 (200) yds; (B) 1 skein, color 484 (teal)—approx 75yd/68m of fingering-weight yarn

Knitting needles: Two 2.5mm (size 2 US) 24"/60cm circular needles or size to obtain gauge

Stitch markers

Scrap yarn

Tapestry needle

## GAUGE

26 sts/36 rnds = 4"/10cm over St st

**NOTE:** Always take time to check your gauge.

### CHART

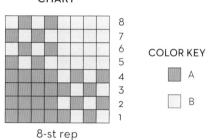

8-st rep

COLOR KEY

▨ A

☐ B

## INSTRUCTIONS

Using the 2 circular method and B, CO 48 (56) sts with 24 (28) sts on each needle. Join, being careful not to twist sts.

### Cuff:

**RNDS 1 AND 2:** *K2, p2, rep from * to end of rnd.

**RNDS 3 AND 4:** *P2, k2, rep from * to end of rnd.

Rep Rnds 1–4 once, then rep Rnds 1 and 2 once more.

### Begin color pattern:

Join A and knit 5 rnds.

With A and B, work Rnds 1–8 of chart, then rep Rnds 1–4 once more.

Cut B.

With A, k 5 (7) rnds.

## Rnd 1:

**NEEDLE 1:** Knit to last 2 sts, pm, k2.

**NEEDLE 2:** Knit.

## Rnd 2 (inc rnd):

**NEEDLE 1:** K to marker, sl m, kfb, k to last 2 sts, kfb, k1.

**NEEDLE 2:** Knit.

**RND 3:** Knit.

**REP RNDS 2 AND 3 FOR 7 (8) TIMES MORE:** Needle 1—40 (44) sts on Needle 1; 22 (26) sts before marker, 18 (20) sts after marker; Needle 2: 24 (28) sts.

## Next rnd:

**NEEDLE 1:** Knit to marker, remove marker, k1, place next 16 (18) sts on scrap yarn for thumb, k1.

**NEEDLE 2:** Knit.

Knit every rnd until mitten hand measures 717 ½ (8 ¼)"/19 (21)cm from thumb opening.

## Shape top:

Next rnd:

**NEEDLE 1:** SSK, k to last 2 sts, k2tog.

**NEEDLE 2:** SSK, k to last 2 sts, k2tog.

Rep this rnd until 8 sts rem on each needle—16 sts.

Use Kitchener stitch to graft rem sts from each needle together.

## Thumb:

Carefully remove scrap yarn and place thumb sts on circular needles, dividing them evenly.

Rejoin yarn to center of thumb closest to body of mitten.

Pick up and k 1 st in the gap before first st on Needle 1, then k 8 (9) sts on Needle 1; k 8 (9) sts on Needle 2, then pick up and k 1 st in gap—18 (20) thumb sts total.

Knit until thumb measures 1¾ (2)"/4 (5) cm.

## Shape thumb top:

**RND 1:** *K2tog, rep from * to end of rnd—9 (10) sts rem.

**RND 2:** *K2tog, rep from * until 5 (5) sts rem, k 0 (1). Break yarn and draw through rem sts to close.

Weave in all ends and block as desired.

### FINISHING:

Make second mitten same as first.

| SUBSTITUTE YARN SWATCH | STATS | YES / **NO** / MAYBE SO |
|---|---|---|

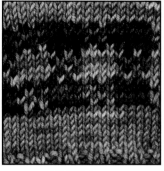

YARN A

**ANCIENT ARTS 100% SUPERWASH MERINO DK**

**Fiber content:** 100% merino wool

**Put-up:** 100g = 220yd/200m

**Price per skein:** $28

**Number of skeins:** 2

**Total cost:** $46

Substitute A is a beautiful hand-dyed semisolid, with elasticity and a great hand. Because it's a superwash yarn with a smoother texture, however, it may not mesh together as well as a stickier yarn. In addition, colorwork purists may find the yarn a bit too soft and processed for their tastes. For those reasons, I've given it a yellow grade, although most knitters will find it a treat to work with.

---

YARN B

**SCHACHENMAYR CATANIA**

**Fiber content:** 100% cotton

**Put-up:** 50g = 137yd/125m

**Price per skein:** $5.49

**Number of skeins:** 2

**Total cost:** $10.98

Substitute B is made of 100 percent mercerized cotton.

Substitute B is made of 100 percent mercerized cotton. While fingering-weight cotton is great for baby items, it's less than ideal for traditional colorwork. The slick surface of the yarn won't mesh together where colors switch, and you may see parts of the floats on the right (public) side of the work. It will also be harder to tension the yarn properly because of the yarn's slipperiness. For this pattern, best to opt for a yarn with at least some wool content and without the unique sheen of mercerization.

---

YARN C

**CASCADE 220 SPORT**

**Fiber content:** 100% wool

**Put-up:** 50g = 137yd/125m

**Price per skein:** $4,75

**Number of skeins:** 3

**Total cost:** $14.25

Traditional stranded patterns are usually made with less-processed, rustic wool, like the sturdy Scandinavian yarn used for the sample. That makes Substitute C the obvious choice from among the three substitutes: it's an all-wool yarn with a "grabby" texture. The untreated wool scales will mesh together to eliminate holes where the different-colored yarns cross in the back.

# Shirl's Shawlette

Who doesn't love lace—especially when it's a graceful swathe you can drape over your shoulders or wrap as a scarf? This delightful shawlette is knit in a heritage Irish yarn that exhibits many of the qualities desirable for **lace knitting**: it is elastic and springy, which makes increases and decreases easy and enhances blocking. It is woolen spun (see page 50), making it light and lofty, which are excellent qualities for a garment that sits on top of your shoulders. Minimally processed, the yarn has a quality that lace maven Brooke Nico calls "stickiness"—the wool's natural scales grab onto one another, giving the pattern a crisp look.

## SKILL LEVEL

**EASY**

## FINISHED MEASUREMENTS

Width (at widest point): 58½"/148cm

Depth (at tallest point): 15"/38cm

## MATERIALS AND TOOLS

Black Water Abbey Yarns 2-Ply Fingering Weight (100% wool; 3oz/85g = 400yds/366m): 1 skein, color Ecru—approx 400yd/366m of fingering-weight yarn

Knitting needles: 4mm (size 6 US) or size to obtain gauge

Removable stitch marker

Tapestry needle

## GAUGE

24 sts/36 rows = 4"/10cm over St st, after blocking

**NOTE:** Always take time to check your gauge.

## INSTRUCTIONS

**NOTE:** Shawlette is knit from side to side.

## Increase Section:

CO 3 sts.

**Row 1(RS):** K1, yo, k2—4 sts.

**Row 2 and all WS rows:** Purl.

**Row 3:** K2, yo, k2—5 sts.

**Row 5:** K3, yo, k2—6 sts.

**Row 7:** K1, ssk, yo, k1, yo, k2—7 sts.

**Row 9:** K2, ssk, yo, k1, yo, k2—8 sts.

**Row 11:** K1, *ssk, yo; rep from * to last 3 sts, k1, yo, k2—1 st inc

**Row 13:** K2, *ssk, yo; rep from * to last 3 sts, k1, yo, k2—1 st inc.

**Row 14:** Purl.

Rep Rows 11–14 until there are 92 sts. Place removable marker in the last row to mark beg of middle section.

## Middle Section:

Work even as follows:

**Next row (RS):** K2, k2tog, yo, k to last 4 sts, k2tog, yo, k2.

**Next row:** (WS): Purl.

**Next row:** K2, yo, ssk, k to last 4 sts, yo, ssk, k2.

**Next row:** Purl.

Rep last 4 rows until middle section measures 10½"/26cm from marker.

### Decrease Section:

**Next row (RS):** K1, *ssk, yo; rep from * to last 3 sts, ssk, k1—1 st dec.

**Next row (WS):** Purl.

**Next row:** K2, *ssk, yo; rep from * to last 3 sts, ssk, k1—1 st dec.

**Next row:** Purl.

Rep last 4 rows until 6 sts rem. Rep first 2 rows of decrease section once more—5 sts.

**Next row (RS):** K2, ssk, k1—4 sts.

**Next row (WS):** Purl.

**Next row:** K1, ssk, k1—3 sts.

BO loosely purlwise.

### FINISHING:

Weave in ends. Block to measurements.

| SUBSTITUTE YARN SWATCH | STATS | YES / **NO** / MAYBE SO |
|---|---|---|

YARN A

**ALCHEMY SILKEN STRAW**

Fiber content: 100% silk

Put-up: 40g = 210yd/192m

Price per skein: $34

Number of skeins: 2

Total cost: $68

Substitute A is an all-silk tape. It feels luxurious against the skin, and the silk's luster adds a depth to the yarn's color. Why did I grade it yellow? Because the flat shape of the yarn may cause bias in the fabric as well as some unevenness in the way the individual stitches lie. Note that blocking should help with this.

YARN B

**BLACK BUNNY FIBERS SUPERWASH SOCK**

Fiber content: 100% superwash wool

Put-up: 100g = 435yd/397m

Price per skein: $24

Number of skeins: 1

Total cost: $24

Lace knitters love working with wool. Its elasticity, the grip of its scales, and its ability to be ruthlessly blocked are a few of the reasons why. Not surprisingly, then, this all-wool sock yarn is graded green. Merino wool has elasticity and spring, and this yarn in particular comes in beautiful hand-dyed colorways that work well with the mesh lace pattern.

YARN C

**AUNT LYDIA'S® CROCHET THREAD™ FASHION™ SIZE 3**

Fiber content: 100% mercerized cotton

Put-up: 150yd/137m

Price per skein: $3.99

Number of skeins: 3

Total cost: $11.97

Substitute C is a mercerized cotton. Its super-smooth surface makes it slippery, while the cotton's lack of elasticity makes this a trickier knit than a more elastic and/or less slick yarn. Lace newbies will probably want to opt for a more traditional lace-knitting yarn to avoid frustration.

# Pebbledash Tunic

Sometimes we overlook the beauty of a simple **textured** pattern, a blend of knits and purls that creates an interesting design element. This tunic features bands of texture around the hem, with a vertical column continuing up the center front. The pattern is echoed in the fold-over collar. A chunky yarn and circular construction help speed the knitting along.

## SKILL LEVEL

**EASY**

## FINISHED MEASUREMENTS:

Bust: 38 (42, 46, 50, 54)"/96½ (106.5, 117, 137)cm

Length: 31 (31½, 32, 32½, 33)"/78.5 (80, 81.5, 82.5, 84)cm

## SIZING:

To fit Women's Small (Medium, Large, X-Large, 1X)

## MATERIALS AND TOOLS

Willow Yarns™ Daily Bulky Yarn (100% superwash wool; 3.5oz/100g = 106yd/97m): 10 (12, 15, 17, 20) skeins, color 0029 Ash—approx 1025 (1270, 1590, 1800, 2120) yds/937 (1164, 1450, 1645, 1940)m of bulky-weight yarn

Knitting needles: 5.5mm (size 9 US) 24"/60cm or 36"/90cm circular needle or size to obtain gauge

5mm (size 8 US) 24"/60cm or 36"/90cm circular needle, or one size smaller than above

6mm (size 10 US) 16"/40cm circular needle, or one size larger than above

Stitch markers

Scrap yarn

Tapestry needle

## GAUGE

14 sts and 20 rnds = 4"/10cm over St st, using 5.5mm (size 9 US) needle

**NOTE:** Always take time to check your gauge.

## INSTRUCTIONS

**Framed Rib Pattern in rounds:**

(over an even number of sts)

RNDS 1 AND 2: Purl.

RNDS 3 AND 4: *K1, p1, rep from * to end of rnd.

RNDS 5 AND 6: Purl.

RNDS 7 AND 8: *P1, k1, rep from * to end of rnd.

Rep Rnds 1–8 for Framed Rib in rnds.

**Center Panel Pattern in rounds:**

(panel of 11 sts)

**Rnds 1 and 2:** P11.

**Rnds 3 and 4:** *K1, p1, rep from * to last st, k1.

**Rnds 5 and 6:** P11.

**Rnds 7 and 8:** P1, k2, [p1, k1] twice, p1, k2, p1.

Rep Rnds 1–8 for Center Panel patt in rnds.

### Center Panel pattern in rows:

(panel of 11 sts)

**Row 1 (RS):** P11.

**Row 2:** K11.

**Row 3:** * K1, p1, rep from * to last st, k1.

**Row 4:** K the knit sts and p the purl sts.

**Rows 5 and 6:** Rep Rows 1 and 2.

**Row 7:** P1, k2, [p1, k1] twice, p1, k2, p1.

**Row 8:** K the knit sts and p the purl sts.

Rep Rows 1–8 for Center Panel patt in rows.

### Body:

With size 9 (5.5mm) needle, CO 67 (73, 81, 87, 95) sts for front, pm, CO 66 (74, 80, 88, 94) sts for back—133 (147, 161, 175, 189) sts. Join, being careful not to twist sts, and place marker for beg of rnd.

**Rnd 1:** Work 28 (31, 35, 38, 42) sts in Framed Rib patt; pm, work 11 sts in Center Panel patt in rnds, pm, work in Framed Rib patt to end of rnd.

Cont in patts as established, slipping markers every rnd until tunic measures 3"/8cm, ending with a pattern Rnd 2.

**Next rnd:** K to first marker; sl m, work in Center Panel patt as established to next marker, k to end of rnd.

Cont in St st and Center Panel patt until tunic measures 23"/58cm or desired length to armholes.

### Divide for front and back:

Place sts for back onto scrap yarn to hold.

### Armhole shaping:

Working in rows on front stitches only, cont as foll:

BO 3 sts at beg of next 2 rows—61 (67, 75, 81, 89) sts.

Cont in patts as established (switching to Center Panel patt in rows) until armhole measures 6 (6½, 7, 7½, 8)"/15.5(16.5, 18, 19, 20.5)cm, ending with a Row 2 or 6 of Center Panel patt.

### Neck shaping:

**Next row (RS):** K to 5 sts before center panel marker, BO 21 sts, removing markers, k to end—20 (23, 27, 30, 34) sts for each shoulder.

### Right Shoulder:

**Next row (WS):** Working on right shoulder only, purl.

**Row 2 (RS):** K1, ssk, k to end.

**Row 3:** P to last 3 sts, p2tog, k1.

Rep Rows 2 and 3 once, then rep Row 2 once more—15 (18, 22, 25, 29) sts.

**Next row (WS):** BO 6 sts, p to end—9 (12, 16, 19, 23) sts.

**Next row:** BO 2 sts, k to end—7 (10, 14, 17, 21) sts.

BO rem sts.

### Left Shoulder:

With WS of work facing, rejoin yarn and p 1 row across left shoulder sts.

**Next row (RS):** K to last 3 sts, k2tog, k1.

**Next row:** P1, p2tog, p to end.

Rep these 2 rows once, then rep first row once more—15 (18, 22, 25, 29) sts.

**Next row (WS):** BO 2 sts, p to end—13 (16, 20, 23, 27) sts.

**Next row:** BO 6 sts, k to end—7 (10, 14, 17, 21) sts.

BO rem sts.

### Back:

Place sts on needle and rejoin yarn, ready to work a WS row. Purl 1 row.

Bind off 3 sts at beg of next 2 rows—60 (68, 74, 82, 88) sts.

Cont in patt as set until underarm measures 7 (7½, 8, 8½, 9)"/18 (19, 20.5, 21.5, 23)cm.

**Next row (RS):** K15 (19, 22, 26, 29), BO next 30 sts, k to end—15 (19, 22, 26, 29) sts rem for each shoulder.

### Left Shoulder:

**Next row (WS):** P to 3 sts before end, p2tog, p1—14 (18, 21, 25, 28) sts.

**Row 2 (RS):** K1, k2tog, k to end—13 (17, 20, 24, 27)sts.

**Next row (WS):** BO 6 sts, p to end.

BO rem sts.

### Right Shoulder:

Rejoin yarn to right shoulder ready to work a WS row.

**Next row (WS):** P1, p2tog, p to end.

**Row 2 (RS):** K to last 3 sts, k2tog, k1.

**Row 3:** Purl.

**Row 4:** BO 6 sts, p to end. BO rem sts.

### Collar:

Turn tunic inside out. With smallest circular needle and WS facing, beg at right shoulder seam, pick up and knit 5 (5, 7, 7, 8) sts along right shoulder, knit across 30 center back sts, pick up and knit 5 (5, 7, 7, 8) sts along left shoulder, pick up and knit 12 (12, 13, 14, 15) sts along left front shoulder, pick up and knit 20 sts across front neck edge, then 12 (12, 13, 14, 15) sts along right front shoulder—84 (84, 90, 92, 96) sts.

**FINISHING:**

Weave in all loose ends. Block pieces gently. Sew shoulder seams.

Change to size 9 (5.5mm) needle and work Framed Rib patt in rounds until collar measures 4"/10cm. Change to larger needle and cont in patt until collar measures 6"/15.5cm, ending with a patt Rnd 2 or 6. BO all sts loosely. Weave in loose ends.

## Armhole edging:

Rejoin yarn at underarm point. With smallest needle and RS facing, pick up and k54 (58, 62, 66, 70) sts evenly around armhole. Purl 2 rnds, then BO all sts knitwise. Rep for second armhole. Weave in all loose ends.

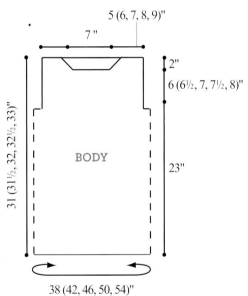

5 (6, 7, 8, 9)"

7 "

2"

6 (6½, 7, 7½, 8)"

31 (31½, 32, 32½, 33)"

BODY

23"

38 (42, 46, 50, 54)"

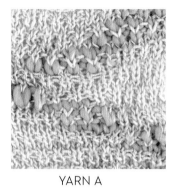

YARN A

### UNIVERSAL YARNS BAMBOO BLOOM HANDPAINTS

**Fiber content:** 48% rayon from bamboo/44% wool/8% acrylic

**Put-up:** 100g = 154yd/XXXm141m

**Price per skein:** $13.50

**Number of skeins:** 7

**Total cost:** $94.50

This pattern was designed to make you think about texture. Accordingly, the sample is knit with a smooth, plied wool yarn that allows the knits and purls to pop. Substitute A has variations in thickness; some areas are nearly unspun, while others are more tightly plied and therefore much thinner. The yarn also has differences in finish, with both matte and shiny areas. While these features enliven the stockinette portions of the tunic, they are likely to overwhelm the textured sections at hem and center front. Note that bamboo is known for its tendency to slide out of shape—a problem with a longer item like a tunic. For all these reasons, I've graded this yarn red (even though I'd love to make a sweater with Bamboo Bloom that lets the yarn be the star!).

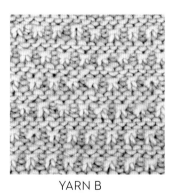

YARN B

### QUINCE & CO. PUFFIN

**Fiber content:** 100% wool

**Put-up:** 100g = 112yd/102m

**Price per skein:** $11.50

**Number of skeins:** 10

**Total cost:** $115

Substitute B is an all-wool single-ply yarn. It has a felted texture, which makes it a bit more durable and less pilly than most singles. This plump yarn has good stitch definition and would be an excellent choice to show off the tunic's texture. The light color makes it easy to see the stitch patterns, an added plus.

### BERROCO ULTRA® ALPACA CHUNKY

**Fiber content:** 50% superfine alpaca/50% wool

**Put-up:** 100g = 131yd/120m

**Price per skein:** $14

**Number of skeins:** 8

**Total cost:** $112

Substitute C is an alpaca/wool blend with a more traditional plied finish. It's a 2-ply and will feel a bit less dense than the felted single used for Substitute B. Substitute C is graded yellow, however, because of its dark color. As you can see by comparing swatches B and C, textural patterns show up best in lighter colors. A quick switch to a different color—the yarn comes in gorgeous heathered shades—and this yarn choice goes from yellow to green.

# Sadie's Shrug

SUBSTITUTION PRINCIPLE: NOVELTY YARNS
• MAY BE HARD TO SUBSTITUTE
• ALWAYS CREATE A SWATCH
• AVOID COMPLEX STITCH PATTERNS

**Novelty yarns** create striking and unique effects in a knitted garment, whether your style tends to the understated or the full-on fabulous. The nature of novelty yarns, however, often makes them tricky to use. Some novelty yarns are made of metallic or synthetic fibers that can be slippery, while others have unusual texture, loops, or "splitty" plies that can catch on your needle. Sadie's Shrug was designed to keep the knitting easy and the construction simple, so you can enjoy the unique qualities of the yarn. Seam the sleeves and you're ready to go, while the yarn—whether sparkly or beaded, adorned with flags or tufts or other doodads—is the star of the show.

## SKILL LEVEL

**EASY**

## FINISHED MEASUREMENTS (AFTER BLOCKING):

Width: Approx 28 (32½, 37, 41½, 46)"/71 (83, 94, 105, 117)cm

Height: Approx 33 (34, 36, 37, 39)"/84 (86, 91, 94, 99)cm

## SIZING:

To fit Women's size Small (Medium, Large, X-Large, 1X)

## MATERIALS AND TOOLS

Lion Brand® Shawl in a Ball® (approx 58% cotton, 39% acrylic, 3% other; 5.3oz/150g = 481yd/440m): 2 (2, 2, 3, 3, 3) skeins, color 207 Feng Shui Grey—approx 600 (775, 950, 1125, 1300)yd/549 (710, 870, 1029, 1190)m of worsted weight yarn

Knitting needles: 5mm (size 8 US) 32"/80cm circular needle or size to obtain gauge (Note: circular needle is used to accommodate large number of stitches; piece is knitted flat, however, rather than in the round.)

Stitch markers

Tapestry needle

Row 8: Purl.

Rep Rows 1–8 for Sadie's Stitch patt.

CO 98 (114, 130, 146, 160) sts loosely. Do not join.

Work in Sadie's Stitch patt until piece measures approx 33 (34, 36, 37, 39)"/84 (86, 91, 94, 99)cm from beg, ending with a Row 5. BO all sts loosely knitwise.

## FINISHING:

Block rectangle, being careful to ensure that the rows of eyelets are straight. Place markers on each side 10½ (10½ 11½, 12, 13)"/27 (27, 29, 30, 33)cm from top of rectangle. With WS together, fold top edge to markers and, working from side edge to center, carefully sew top edge using mattress st carefully to the main part of garment 8 (8, 8.5, 9, 9)"/20 (20, 22, 23, 23)cm on each side, leaving center of shrug open.

## GAUGE:

14 sts/20 rows = 4"/10cm over Sadie's Stitch patt after blocking.

**NOTE:** Always take time to check your gauge.

## INSTRUCTIONS

**Sadie's Stitch Pattern:**

(over an even number of sts)

Row 1 (RS): Knit.

Row 2 (WS): Knit.

Row 3: K2, *k2tog, yo, rep from * to last st, k2.

Rows 4 AND 5: Knit.

Row 6: Purl.

Row 7: Knit.

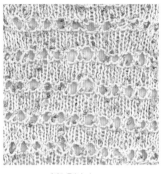

YARN A

### FILATURA DI CROSA SOLARE

**Fiber content:** 77% cotton/17% viscose/6% polyamide

**Put-up:** 100g = 150yd/137m

**Price per skein:** $10.99

**Number of skeins:** 4

**Total cost:** $43.96

Here's another pattern with lots of flexibility for substituting. It was tough to pick only three yarns to compare, since there are so many interesting novelty yarns. The sample is knit in a gradient-style yarn with a thick-and-thin texture; a slightly brushed finish adds a dreamy, hazy look. Substitute A is a cotton blend with a multicolored ply, textural differences, and nubs. It's a more festive look, and the mostly cotton yarn makes it wearable all year round.

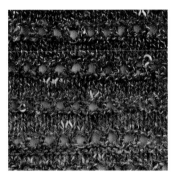

YARN B

### NORO KUJAKU

**Fiber content:** 85% wool/15% polyester

**Put-up:** 100g = 100yd/91m

**Price per skein:** $9.99

**Number of skeins:** 2

**Total cost:** $19.98

Substitute B is an unusual offering from Noro Yarns, known for their vivid colors and unusual color combinations. While Noro is known for self-striping yarns, this yarn featured a tightly twisted wool strand with a multicolored poly binder. The yarn also contains areas where the poly binder is wrapped around the strand entirely. The effect is less ethereal and very bold.

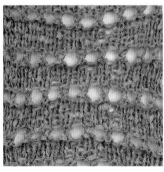

YARN C

### BERROCO LINUS®

**Fiber content:** 50% acrylic/20% linen/18% nylon/12% rayon/viscose

**Put-up:** 50g = 159yd/145m

**Price per skein:** $10.99

**Number of skeins:** 4

**Total cost:** $43.96

Substitute C is a tape yarn with linen content; the width of the tape varies slightly, and the tape has a very loose, railroad-style construction. This choice has a more casual feel, although changing color to a deeper shade would amp up the drama. Like the other two choices, Substitute C is graded green since the guiding factor will be personal taste.

# Little Bird Slouchy Hat

**Hand-painted yarns** present their own unique challenges when it comes time to substitute. This simple, textured hat uses a slip-stitch pattern that works well with many types of hand-paints. The sample is shown in a delightful speckled colorway. I love how the individual flecks look like confetti sprinkled randomly across the top. Try other types of colorways—semisolids, muted color combinations, vibrant mixes, even a gradient—to compare how different styles of dyeing result in different finished effects.

## SKILL LEVEL

**EASY**

## FINISHED MEASUREMENTS

Circumference to fit: 16–18 (18–20, 20–22)"/41–46 (46–51, 51–56)cm

Length: 9½ (10, 10½)"/24 (25, 26.5)cm

## SIZING:

To fit Adult Small (Medium, Large)

**NOTE:** Brim stretches to fit a variety of sizes.

## MATERIALS AND TOOLS

Hedgehog Fibres Merino DK (100% superwash merino; 4oz/115g = 220yd/201m): 1 skein, color Fool's Gold—approx 160 (180, 200)yd/146 (165, 183)m of DK weight yarn

Knitting needles: 4mm (size 6 US) 16"/40cm circular needle or size to obtain gauge

Set of 4mm (size 6 US) double-pointed needles or second circular needle

3.5mm (size 4 US) 16"/40cm circular needle or two sizes smaller than above

Stitch marker

Tapestry needle

## GAUGE

20 sts /32 rnds = 4"/10cm over Slip Stitch patt using larger needle

## INSTRUCTIONS

### Rib Pattern:

(multiple of 4 stitches)

RND 1: *K1, p1, rep from * to end of rnd.

RND 2: *Sl 1 wyib, p1, k1 p1, rep from * to end of rnd.

Rep Rnds 1 and 2 for Rib patt.

### Slip Stitch Pattern:

(over an even number of stitches)

RND 1: *K1, yo, sl wyif, rep from * to end of rnd.

RND 2: *K1, p2tog, rep from * to end of rnd.

RNDS 3 AND 4: Knit.

Rep Rnds 1–4 for Slip Stitch patt.

Using smaller needles, CO 104 (112, 120) sts. Join, being careful not to twist sts, and place marker for beg of rnd.

Work in Rib patt until hat measures 1½"/4cm from beg, ending with a Rnd 1.

Knit 1 rnd.

Change to larger needle and work in Slip Stitch patt until hat measures 8½ (9, 9½)"/22 (23, 24)cm from beg, ending with a Rnd 2.

### Top Shaping:

DEC RND: *K2tog; rep from * to end of rnd—52 (56, 60) sts.

Knit 1 rnd.

Work Rnds 1 and 2 of Slip Stitch patt.

DEC RND: *K2tog; rep from * to end of rnd—26 (28, 30) sts.

REP DEC RND ONCE MORE—13 (14, 15) STS.

NEXT RND: *K2tog, rep to last st, k1 (0, 1)—7 (8, 9) sts.

Cut yarn, leaving a long tail. Thread tail through rem sts to close. Weave in ends and block as desired.

YARN A

### KOIGU KERSTI

**Fiber content:** 100% merino wool

**Put-up:** 50g = 114yd/105m

**Price per skein:** $14

**Number of skeins:** 2

**Total cost:** $28

Discover the wonderful world of hand-paints with this fun and easy cap. The original yarn features a speckled effect, along with pops of multiple colors. The Slip Stitch pattern helps move the colors around and adds subtle texture. Substitute A is a crepe-style merino yarn. It has terrific stitch definition and is a pleasure to knit with. By using a hand-dyed solid color, the net effect is more muted than the speckled yarn, but it works beautifully.

YARN B

### COLINETTE TAO

**Fiber content:** 100% silk

**Put-up:** 50g = 126yd/115m

**Price per skein:** $27.50

**Number of skeins:** 2

**Total cost:** $55

Substitute B is a luscious multicolored all-silk yarn. The colorway is relatively quiet, with soft sages and cream, but it still has plenty of visual interest. I graded this yarn red, however, because of its incredibly delicate structure. The soft fibers and loose twist mean it will show wear very easily. In addition, silk's inelasticity and glossy surface means it won't hold ribbing very well and is likely to stretch out of shape.

YARN C

### BLACK BUNNY FIBERS COTTON GIN

**Fiber content:** 52% cotton/48% acyrlic

**Put-up:** 100g = 317yd/290m

**Price per skein:** $14

**Number of skeins:** 1

**Total cost:** $14

Substitute C features a somewhat brighter array of colors that may pool a bit, although the stitch pattern will help minimize some of the pooling. It's a cotton/acrylic blend: the cotton is inelastic, although the acrylic content is likely to help the yarn keep its shape. I've graded this yellow since you'll want to make sure the ribbed brim stays in place (perhaps knitting it with a smaller needle size) and to keep an eye on pooling or other unwanted color effects.

# RESOURCES/ BIBLIOGRAPHY

Every knitter should have at least one comprehensive reference book in their library. These are my favorites:

Bliss, Debbie. *The Knitter's Book of Knowledge*. New York: Lark Crafts, 2015.

Editors of Vogue Knitting Magazine. *Vogue Knitting: The Ultimate Knitting Book.* New York: Sixth&Spring Books, 2018.

Hemmons Hiatt, June. *The Principles of Knitting*. New York: Touchstone, 2012.

Stanley, Montse. *Reader's Digest Knitter's Handbook.* Pleasantville, NY: Reader's Digest, 1999.

For more information about fiber content and yarn construction, in addition to the above, I recommend:

Ekarius, Carol. *The Fleece & Fiber Sourcebook*. North Adams, MA: Storey Publishing, 2011.

Fournier, Jane, and Nola Fournier. *In Sheep's Clothing.* New York: Interweave Press, 2013.

Parkes, Clara. *The Knitter's Book of Wool.* New York: Potter Craft, 2009.

———. *The Knitter's Book of Yarn.* New York: Potter Craft, 2011.

Smith, Beth. *The Spinner's Book of Fleece.* North Adams, MA: Storey Publishing, 2014.

For information about specific types of yarn:

Sulcoski, Carol J. *Lace Yarn Studio*. New York: Lark Crafts, 2015.
———. *Self-Striping Yarn Studio*. New York: Lark Crafts, 2016.
———. *Sock Yarn Studio*. New York: Lark Crafts, 2012.

For when you can't match the category or want to do your own thing:

Leapman, Melissa. *6000+ Pullover Possibilities*. New York: Sixth&Spring Books, 2017.

If you want to delve further into the world of gauge, I highly recommend Pattty Lyons's gauge class, taught at many yarn shows and local yarn shops. Learn more at pattylyons.com.

# KNITTING ABBREVIATIONS

| | | | |
|---|---|---|---|
| alt | alternate | patt | pattern |
| approx | approximately | pm | place marker |
| beg | begin; beginning | p2tog | purl 2 stitches together; single purl decrease |
| bet | between | | |
| BO | bind off | prev | previous |
| cat | category | pwise | purlwise |
| CC | contrasting color | rem | remain(ing)/remainder |
| CN | cable needle | rep | repeat(s)/repeating |
| CO | cast on | RH | right-hand needle |
| cont | continue | rnd | round |
| dec | decrease/decreased | RS | right side (public side) |
| foll | following | sl | slip |
| inc | increase/increased | sl1k | slip one stitch knitwise |
| k | knit | slp | slip one stitch purlwise |
| kfb | knit 1 in front and back of same stitch; single increase | sl m | slip marker |
| | | ssk | slip 2 stitches knitwise, knit these two stitches together through back loops; single left-leaning decrease |
| k2tog | knit two stitches together; single right-leaning decrease | | |
| kwise | knitwise | st(s) | stitch/stitches |
| LH | left-hand | St st | Stockinette stitch |
| m | marker | WS | wrong side |
| MC | main color | wyib | with working yarn held at back of work |
| p | purl | | |
| | | YO | yarnover |

# YARN CLASSIFICATION CHART

| CATEGORY 0 | CATEGORY 1 | CATEGORY 2 | CATEGORY 3 | CATEGORY 4 | CATEGORY 5 | CATEGORY 6 | CATEGORY 7 |
|---|---|---|---|---|---|---|---|
| Lace | Superfine | Fine | Light | Medium | Bulky | Super Bulky | Jumbo |
| Lace-weight, cobweb, crochet thread, 2-ply | Fingering, sock, 4-ply, baby | Sport, baby | DK (double-knitting), light worsted | Worsted, light vs. heavy worsted, aran | Chunky, bulky | Superchunky, polar | Arm knitting yarn |
| 8 or more sts per inch but variable | 7–8 sts per inch | 6–7 sts per inch | 5–6 sts per inch | 4–5 sts per inch | 3–4 sts per inch | 2–3 sts per inch | Fewer than 2 sts per inch |
| US 0 or smaller (variable – US 4-9) | US 0–3 | US 3–5 | US 5–7 | US 7–9 | US 9–13 | US 13–17 | Larger than US 17 |
| More than 210 yds/50g | 180–210 yds/50g | 150–180 yds/50g | 120–150 yds/50g | 90–120 yds/50g | 60–90 yds/50g | 30–60 yds/50g | Fewer than 30 yds/50g |

# WORKSHEETS

**YARN:** _____

FIBER CONTENT: _____

PUT-UP: _____

PRICE PER SKEIN: _____

QUANTITY OF SKEINS: _____

TOTAL COST: _____

NOTES: _____

_____

**YARN:** _____

FIBER CONTENT: _____

PUT-UP: _____

PRICE PER SKEIN: _____

QUANTITY OF SKEINS: _____

TOTAL COST: _____

NOTES: _____

_____

# YARN: _____

FIBER CONTENT: _____

PUT-UP: _____

PRICE PER SKEIN: _____

QUANTITY OF SKEINS: _____

TOTAL COST: _____

NOTES: _____

_____

# YARN: _____

FIBER CONTENT: _____

PUT-UP: _____

PRICE PER SKEIN: _____

QUANTITY OF SKEINS: _____

TOTAL COST: _____

NOTES: _____

_____

# INDEX

# ACKNOWLEDGMENTS

Without the attention and care of editor Wendy Williams and tech editor Lori Steinberg, this book would not be here. I owe them a special debt of gratitude for their patience beyond measure. (I can't believe you didn't smack me upside the head several times.) Thanks to photographer Lynne Harty for the gorgeous photographs and to the entire team at Lark Crafts for their hard work, as well as to my agent, Linda. I wish I could buy you all a drink!

To all the students I've had in my classes over the years: Thanks for making my classes fun and for teaching me so much. Your feedback, questions, and comments form an integral part of this book.

I am blessed to have the support of family and friends whom I'm not always sure I deserve. My mom and my brother have been in my corner in ways I never imagined I'd need—I love you so much. My friends Brooke, Patty, and Melissa are sisters of the heart who have (literally) saved my life time and time again. Elizabeth is a friend whose worth is beyond measure, while my lunchtime knitters keep me sane and inspire me. Kathy, Barb, Trisha, the band moms, my ragtag band of online pals, fluffball Boris—you are all an important part of my world and help keep me anchored and laughing at the absurdity of it all. Truly, I am very grateful for all of you.

And to James, Nick, and Grace: I could not possibly love or appreciate you more. Thank you for making my world infinitely brighter and better.

# ABOUT THE AUTHOR

Carol J. Sulcoski first learned to knit as a child long ago, but it didn't stick. She returned to the craft as an adult and has been obsessed ever since. Although Carol works by day as an attorney with a large global law firm, she knits whenever she has a chance, even if it's only while commuting on the train. This is Carol's seventh book; look for her Studio series, also by Lark Crafts, and indulge your love of knitting factoids with *Knitting Ephemera* (Sixth&Spring 2016). Carol's designs have been published in many books and magazines, and she also publishes her own patterns under the Black Bunny Fibers name.

In addition to designing, Carol has written technical and historical articles about knitting for magazines including *Vogue Knitting*, *Debbie Bliss Magazine*, *Jane Austen Knits*, *Yarn Market News*, and the *Craft Industry Alliance Journal*, to name a few. She hand dyes yarn as Black Bunny Fibers, selling at select knitting shops and at fiber festivals. Carol lives with her three nearly grown-up children and her majestic cat outside Philadelphia. Learn more at www.blackbunnyfibers.com.

31901064487996